DOCTOR TO THE NORTH

Footprints Series
JANE ERRINGTON, Editor

The life stories of individual women and men who were participants in interesting events help nuance larger historical narratives, at times reinforcing those narratives, at other times contradicting them. The Footprints series introduces extraordinary Canadians, past and present, who have led fascinating and important lives at home and throughout the world.

The series includes primarily original manuscripts but may consider the English-language translation of works that have already appeared in another language. The editor of the series welcomes inquiries from authors. If you are in the process of completing a manuscript that you think might fit into the series, please contact her, care of McGill-Queen's University Press, 3430 McTavish Street, Montreal, QC H3A 1X9.

Blatant Injustice
The Story of a Jewish Refugee from Nazi Germany Imprisoned in Britain and Canada during World War II
Walter W. Igersheimer
Edited and with a foreword by Ian Darragh

Against the Current
Boris Ragula
Memoirs

Margaret Macdonald
Imperial Daughter
Susan Mann

My Life at the Bar and Beyond
Alex K. Paterson

Red Travellers
Jeanne Corbin and Her Comrades
Andrée Lévesque

The Teeth of Time
Remembering Pierre Elliott Trudeau
Ramsay Cook

The Greater Glory
Thirty-seven Years with the Jesuits
Stephen Casey

Doctor to the North
Thirty Years Treating Heart Disease among the Inuit
John H. Burgess

DOCTOR TO THE NORTH

Thirty Years Treating Heart Disease among the Inuit

J O H N   H .   B U R G E S S

McGILL-QUEEN'S UNIVERSITY PRESS

Montreal & Kingston · London · Ithaca

© McGill-Queen's University Press 2008

ISBN 978-0-7735-3431-5

Legal deposit third quarter 2008
Bibliothèque nationale du Québec

Printed in Canada on acid-free paper that is 100% ancient forest free
(100% post-consumer recycled), processed chlorine free.

McGill-Queen's University Press acknowledges the support of the Canada Council for
the Arts for our publishing program. We also acknowledge the financial support of the
Government of Canada through the Book Publishing Industry Development Program
(BPIDP) for our publishing activities.

Library and Archives Canada Cataloguing in Publication

Burgess, John H., 1933–
Doctor to the North : thirty years treating heart disease among the Inuit /
John H. Burgess.

(Footprints series 8)
Includes bibliographical references.
ISBN 978-0-7735-3431-5

1. Burgess, John H., 1933– . 2. Inuit–Health and hygiene–Nunavut–Baffin Region.
3. Inuit–Health and hygiene–Québec (Province)–Nunavik. 4. Cardiovascular system–
Diseases–Canada, Northern. 5. Heart–Diseases–Canada, Northern. 6. Inuit–Medical
care–Nunavut–Baffin Region. 7. Inuit–Medical care–Québec (Province)–Nunavik.
8. Medical care–Canada, Northern. 9. Cardiologists–Canada, Northern–Biography.
I. Title. II. Series.

R464.B898A3 2008   616.1'20092   C2008-901806-0

This book was designed and typeset by studio oneonone in New Baskerville 10/14.5

For Andrea
She always wanted me to write this book.

Contents

Colour section follows 134

Acknowledgments | x

1 The Long Road to an MD | 3

2 Expanding Horizons during Postgraduate Training | 18

3 Return to North America | 32

4 Cardiologist at the Montreal General Hospital and
   McGill University | 40

5 My Road to the Presidency of the Royal College | 44

6 Doctor to the North | 47

7 History of the Eastern Canadian Inuit | 59

8 History of Eastern Canadian Inuit Health Care | 75

9 Congenital Heart Disease | 83

10 Valvular Heart Disease | 96

11 Infective Endocarditis | 111

CONTENTS

12 Pulmonary Heart Disease | 115

13 Cardiomyopathy | 118

14 Coronary Artery Disease | 122

15 Auyuittuq Park: An Arctic Holiday | 133

16 The Future | 145

17 Transitions | 150

    Notes | 161

    Index | 165

Acknowledgments

My wife, Andrea, was the driving force behind my beginning this autobiography. Following her death in April 2001, my children, Willa, Cynthia, Lynn, and John, provided me with the support to carry on with my career and to get started on the manuscript. Cynthia and Lynn particularly helped me with its organization, content, and revisions.

Dr Phil Gold, former physician-in-chief at the Montreal General Hospital, and Dr Jacques Genest, director of Cardiology at the McGill University Health Centre, read early versions and encouraged me to continue. Dr Maurice Godin, associate director of the Division of Cardiology, spent many hours covering my MGH duties during my northern visits.

Professor Desmond Morton, past director of the Institute for Canadian Studies at McGill University, reviewed my early manuscript and recommended significant changes.

Jonah Kelly, a former patient of mine in Iqaluit and long-time CBC radio announcer there, confirmed that I had not made any significant errors in Inuit history and that my patient descriptions were appropriate.

John Labelle, medical photographer at the Montreal General Hospital, transformed my 35 mm slides into digital form and created the prints necessary for publication.

I am particularly indebted to Professor John Zucchi, senior editor of McGill-Queen's University Press. He asked me to revise the manuscript from a simple memoir of my thirty years as consultant cardiologist to the Arctic to a more complete autobiography. I also wish to thank Joan McGilvray and Maureen Garvie, my copy editor, who greatly improved the final manuscript.

I acknowledge generous grants from an anonymous donor and other foundations that made the publication possible.

DOCTOR TO THE NORTH

1

The Long Road to an MD

My father, John Frederick Burgess, was a doctor. He graduated from the University of Toronto in 1913 and immediately entered surgical training. Unfortunately, this was interrupted by the onset of the First World War. He was twenty-five years old when he joined the 5th Field Ambulance, and he was sent to France one year later. His first major campaign was the battle of Passchendaele beginning in July 1917 – known as the "Battle of the Mud." While moving forward during the famous Canadian offensive of October 1918, the ambulance in which he was riding was hit by a shell. One of the driver's arms was severed, and the other surgeon in the front seat died immediately. Shrapnel hit my father in the left arm. Somehow the driver was able to get through the rain and mud to a casualty clearing station. Although my father never talked of his wartime experiences, my mother told me that the driver was awarded a high military honour.

Because of the filthy conditions and the lack of antibiotics, my father's wound, initially below the elbow, soon became infected. Gangrene was already setting in before he was evacuated to the Royal Free Hospital in London ten days later. Surgeons there attempted to save the arm, but after several weeks of revising amputations higher, my father ended up with a stump too short for an artificial limb. His surgical career ended. He must have wondered if he could still be a doctor – there were not many options for a man with one arm.

After receiving the Order of the British Empire and a handwritten letter from King George V thanking him for his wartime services, my father returned to Ottawa, taking a desk job with the Armed Forces Pension Board. There he met and married my mother, who encouraged him not to give up on a career in medicine. He decided to become a dermatologist. He and my mother lived for a year in Vienna and another in London while he trained with the best practitioners in the field. They returned to Canada in 1921, where my father was offered a position at the Montreal General Hospital (MGH) and McGill University.

My baptismal certificate – birth certificates were rare in a predominantly Roman Catholic province, where it was assumed that every newborn would be baptized – states that I was born to Dr John Frederick Burgess and Willa Reta McGinness on 24 May 1933. However, as I was adopted by a private arrangement through one of my father's colleagues, this document was obviously fudged. I am sure I was born in May 1933, but I was always suspicious that my parents picked the 24th. As a child I thought that my classmates got a holiday because of my birthday. I later learned that it was Queen Victoria's birthday as well.

My father was a leader – I was told years later that he was one of the youngest majors in the Canadian Army – and a fighter. I admired him tremendously for his determination to succeed at everything he tried. He taught me by example about perseverance. One thing he had to concede he couldn't do with one arm was tying his shoes, an essential service I provided every morning. He played tennis, flipping the ball into the air with his left stump, and he also played golf, scoring in the low eighties. I remember playing with him as a youngster and seeing the looks of astonishment on the other players' faces as they watched him drive more than two hundred yards off the tee. I could never beat him. As I grew older, I easily out-drove him, but my shots would be in the rough while his were always in the middle of the fairway. He was also an excellent putter; he always emphasized that half the strokes in a game of golf took place on the green. He was a very frustrating opponent.

His main hobby in his later years was photography. It started through his making teaching slides of various skin problems in his office and clinic. Later he spent his summer vacations digging up various fungi in the woods and bringing them back to a table at our country home to photograph. He would spend hours arranging them at different angles against various backgrounds. His winter evenings were occupied by sending coloured slides to various North American exhibitions where he often won prizes.

He was pleased when I showed an interest in his hobby. Together, we set up a darkroom in a converted coal-room in our basement and were soon developing and enlarging black and white photos. We were about to move to colour processing when my father died suddenly. My interest in photography went with him, only to be awakened during my travels in Great Britain, California, and especially later in the Canadian Arctic.

EARLY CAREER AMBITIONS

As an only child I was never pushed by my father towards a career in medicine, although he nudged me in that direction. However, during my junior high school years, I planned to be a chemist. I bought textbooks and set up a chemistry set in the basement. Most of the time I made useless compounds. My only real triumph was the production of oxygen and hydrogen by electrodes in inverted test tubes under water in one of my mother's frying pans. As the great French chemist Lavoisier recognized, oxygen supported combustion, and the hydrogen exploded when lit with a match. My mother confiscated the frying pan after the experiment.

However, chemistry was a lonely activity. As I became older and met my father's patients, friends, and colleagues, I realized how much they admired him and I saw the influence he had on younger colleagues' careers. It was my appreciation of the importance of the care he took with his patients and the number of different people he came into contact with every day that turned me towards medicine.

I watched him perform in his dermatological practice only once. His nurse-secretary was ill, and I went to his office after school on several days to help him. I was responsible for patient reception, but I did look on while he dexterously filled syringes with local anesthetic with one hand and removed various growths from his patients' skin. He was head of the dermatology department at MGH for twenty-five years. I knew my father was internationally famous, as he had published about a hundred medical papers and was clinical professor of dermatology at the time of his retirement in 1951.

ON TO UNDERGRADUATE STUDIES AT MCGILL

I finished first in my class at the end of high school and because of my athletic activities was awarded the Senior All Round Cup. The caption under my picture in the yearbook reads: "John plans to become a doctor, but I doubt if any of his classmates will be his patients." Actually, several have been.

The transition from the small pond of high school to the large academic pond at McGill University was difficult. Classes were huge, with 250 or more students, and impersonal. I listened to the lecturers in the large halls, rarely looking up because of the need I felt to transcribe every word in longhand. No handouts were offered, a fact I would recall years later when I became a teacher. There seemed no place to turn for help except the standard textbooks, often written by the professors themselves.

I majored in chemistry and mathematics, the latter because I thought it was the only way to get grades in the 90s that would improve my chances of later medical school acceptance. My chemistry courses were difficult and showed that I was not cut out for a career in that field. I managed to pass, but not with honours. I particularly remember the organic chemistry labs – six hours per week. As in most undergraduate courses, the laboratories were supervised by postgraduate students; I never encountered the professor, except in the presence of many other students in the lecture theatre. Pairs of students were presented with unknown compounds to analyze. If the results were not close enough to the answer, the analysis, which took at least three hours, would have to be repeated. I began to think that I would never complete this required pre-medical course. These early experiences convinced me in later years that small-group teaching should be used as much as possible.

A second-year physics course particularly designed for pre-med students was smaller, but again the laboratory work seemed unrelated to anything I wanted to do later in life. My only lasting memory is that the classes were held on an upper floor of the old Physics Building, where Lord Rutherford originally split the atom.

So as not to be totally immersed in science, I wanted to take some arts courses and took a full year's course in Shakespeare taught by a spellbinding lecturer, Professor George Ian Duthie.

This taught me an appreciation of the plays, especially the tragedies, that has lasted all my life, but again my contact with the teacher was remote.

My most memorable undergraduate course was Greek and Roman Literature in Translation. There were less than twenty students in a small upper room in the Arts Building. The teacher was Professor Woodhouse, a small, soft-spoken, and kindly man. He would bring a few dozen books from his personal library to each class and was quite comfortable lending them out for a week or two. Many years later one of my medical colleagues was amazed that I made my own books readily available to students. For the first time I felt able to question the professor after class and to discuss the results of my assignments. The course was designed for future postgraduate students in the arts. I think Professor Woodhouse was a little surprised to find a pre-medical student had achieved higher marks than his literary majors. He asked me with a smile if I really wanted to pursue a career in medicine, but he supposed that it wouldn't hurt a doctor to have a grounding in the humanities.

My father died suddenly at home in 1953 before the end of my third year of science. I came home one day to find a policeman's hat on the hall table and my mother telling me, "He's gone." I was nineteen years old and stunned that the most important person in my life, the man who was going to guide me to a career in medicine, was no longer there. My mother and I spent a tearful evening alone – we had no relatives in Montreal – wondering about our future. My father, the fifth child of a schoolteacher in a small Ontario town, had no inheritance. His total assets came from twenty-five years of dermatological practice. Would my mother and I be able to stay in our Westmount home and maintain our cherished summer place in Vermont? Would I still be able to go on to medical school as I had planned?

Author's parents, Fred and Reta Burgess, 1953

Fortunately, there were no mortgages or debts. The day after my father died, a man from the trust company came and told my mother she would have an income of $3,500 per year. That would cover our taxes, food, and other essentials. I could earn enough at a summer job to cover my university fees and books and would live rent free at home. A few days later an official from the Department of Veterans Affairs visited. Sitting at our dining-room table, he informed my mother that she would receive $100 monthly tax free for the rest of her life because of my father's war wound – not a large compensation for the loss of a surgeon's arm, but it certainly helped.

I had planned to apply to medical school after third year science, but with my extreme sense of loss, and exams only a few weeks away, I decided to complete a full undergraduate degree. This proved a good decision, as it allowed me more elective courses in the humanities. My final grades were adequate, but I worried that they might not be high enough for medical school acceptance. My mother and I were thrilled when the confirmation letter arrived, although some of my less tactful acquaintances suggested that my acceptance was due more to my father's faculty position and reputation than to my own academic achievements.

MEDICAL SCHOOL AT MCGILL

The transition from science to medicine was as great as that from high school to university. There were 115 students in my first year class. Only three were women, whereas now female students account for over 50 per cent of present-day classes. Nearly half of the students in my class were American, as McGill had a reputation equal to that of the top American schools, at about one-fifth the tuition fees. I had only two or three friends from my undergraduate days. We all quickly made new friends, not through fraternities or clubs but from being partners around the anatomy tables and other laboratories. Most of my classmates with whom I have remained in touch now live in the United States.

On our first day the dean greeted us. I remember his admonition that from day one we must uphold the dignity of our chosen profession. Jackets and ties were to be worn on all occasions except for when we wore long (and clean) white coats in the laboratories. Hair and fingernails were to be kept clean and short. My mother was pleased that I no longer would be leaving home in an open-necked shirt and slacks. The inspiring part of the dean's welcome was his statement that in view of the high entrance standards, we were all expected to graduate – a prophecy that came true for all but two of us.

FIRST YEAR

First year medical school was drudgery, all memory work with little requirement for critical thinking. I particularly remember the anatomy laboratories. On our second day on a hot September morning we were ushered into a large upstairs room smelling strongly of formaldehyde and containing fifteen emaciated cadavers. Professor C.P. Martin apologized "for the shortage of material" – we were four students on each side of our designated body. We would spend about nine hours weekly during the first year dissecting this body following a manual. Every few weeks there would be an "anatomy spot" during which we would spend one minute each at about twenty tables, identifying designated structures. The stress of these exams was overwhelming. The one redeeming feature of learning so much detailed anatomy that we might never use was Professor Martin's full-class lectures. A Dublin graduate with an engaging Irish accent, he drew anatomical structures on the blackboard with coloured chalk. Frequently he would interrupt his lectures with questions to the class. He had been wounded during the Great War, losing a piece of the visual

Author with father and mother, 1953

(rear) part of his brain. He covered the defect in his skull with a distinctive black patch. We learned that he could not see the left side of the class, so that if we had not done our homework, we would struggle to get a seat in that area of the room.

Another new experience was histology, the microscopic study of body structures. We were required to reproduce with coloured pencils what we saw under a microscope. I had never done well in art and felt particularly disadvantaged in this performance. The professor, C.P. Leblond, was a world-famous researcher, renowned for his use of radioactive substances in the study of glandular function, but several generations of medical students remember him for his detailed and colourful blackboard drawings of the external anatomy of the male and female reproductive systems. He would draw the organs, then step back and say, "Perhaps I should be a bit more generous."

Courses in physiology and biochemistry rounded out my first year. The laboratory exercises were interesting, and the professors were masters in the art of whole-class lectures. However, as I had not yet seen a patient, I could not understand the relevance to clinical medicine of the copious amounts of material I memorized four hours nightly. A pretty second-year nursing student at the Montreal General Hospital, a woman who would later become my wife, convinced me that what I was trying to learn would have some use in my future career.

At the end of my first year of medical school I was ranked seventy-eighth in my class. This result did not suggest that I would have a career in academic medicine.

SECOND YEAR

My second year was dominated by pathology – the study of disease – and an introduction to clinical medicine – patients. I began to learn about abnormal instead of normal body chemistry and function. Cognitive skills began to replace memory work.

Professor Lyman Duff, an international authority on atherosclerosis (hardening of the arteries), was one of the outstanding teachers at McGill. In addition to his whole-class lectures, he would hold clinical-pathological conferences during which students would be summoned down to the front of the amphitheatre, shown an organ such as a heart, kidney, or lung, and asked to describe the disease. We all attended despite the fact that these sessions were held from 11:00 A.M. until 1:00 P.M. every Saturday. Today even the best lecturers would have difficulty in getting a minority of students to Saturday-morning sessions.

Professor Duff was a heavy cigarette smoker before the habit was recognized as a major cause of lung cancer and heart disease. One Saturday morning he did not appear, and we soon learned that he was in hospital with lung cancer that had spread to his brain. Virtually every smoker in my class, including myself, immediately quit. The impact of losing this great teacher was so powerful that we did not need to await definitive proof of the serious health effects of smoking.

I saw my first patients during the latter half of my second year and began to learn the art of taking a patient's history and performing a physical examination. I began to realize that although it had taken nearly two years, I had made the right career choice. For Christmas of 1956, Andrea, my wife-to-be, gave me a copy of *Heart Disease* by the great Dr Paul Dudley White of Boston. I studied the book – not exactly bedtime reading – over Christmas and decided that I would become a heart specialist.

My class ranking moved up to forty-sixth at the end of second year.

THIRD YEAR

Sir William Osler (1849–1919) was the greatest physician of his day, perhaps of all time. He was successively a professor of Medicine at McGill, the University of Philadelphia, and Johns Hopkins and finally Regius Professor of Medicine at Oxford, England. His textbook *The Principles and Practice of Medicine* was the standard for undergraduate and postgraduate students for decades. But his major contribution to medical teaching was that he brought students onto the hospital wards. Prior to his influence in the late 1880s, medical students had not been allowed near patients until after graduation.

During my third year I was assigned patients to "work up," visiting them on my own, eliciting the stories of their illness, performing physical examinations and synthesizing these findings in an attempt to arrive at my diagnoses and plans of investigation and management. Being alone with a sick person for an hour or two was initially both a nerve-wracking and a maturing experience. Along with other small groups of students, I would present my patients to an assigned staff physician. In the McGill tradition my mentors were usually doctors in private practice who devoted many hours to teaching in return for the privilege of admitting their patients to a McGill hospital. I was not yet part of a hospital team, but I was beginning to feel like a doctor.

After my third year of medical school, I ranked third in my class. This was a great improvement over prior years. reflecting my growing fascination with medical practice.

SUMMERS

I spent my vacations during medical school working at a summer hotel, the Ojibway, in Georgian Bay. The pay was enough to cover my tuition and books, and there was nowhere to spend it. The hotel was on an island twelve kilometres from Pointe au Baril.

The first summer I drove a boat, ferrying hotel guests to and from the mainland. Towards the end of the season, taking a passenger to catch a 2:00 A.M. train, I drove the boat onto a shoal. We sat out the night high and dry but uninjured, until we were rescued by a nearby islander at daylight. The next year I was promoted to a desk job as accountant: any future mistakes could be financially significant for the hotel management, but not hazardous to my health or that of paying guests.

The hotel had a doctor who was available to the staff, guests, and the many cottagers on surrounding islands. I would frequently drive him to his island house calls and even assist him during minor surgical procedures. I once fainted helping him remove two litres of fluid from the chest cavity of a man with terminal cancer. Both the doctor and the patient must have wondered if I had the stuff to become a physician.

My most poignant memory was being called to the hotel laundry to find that a young immigrant employee had commit-

ted suicide by hanging herself. It was the first time I had encountered death on my own. I controlled my emotions long enough
to cover her and call the police. Several close observers called
me "Doctor." I did not correct them.

Most of my early patients were animals. I was asked to remove
porcupine quills from a dog's mouth, but when the frightened
animal bit my hand, I decided that a consultation with a veteri-
narian on the mainland was the best course of action. A young
boy brought his cat with a fishhook in its belly. I asked the youngster to hold the cat while I attempted to push the barb through
the skin and remove the hook. This time it was the owner who
was frightened. He let go of the cat, who promptly took a piece
of skin off the back of my hand. I decided to retire from veteri-
nary practice and await my graduation before attempting any
more medical procedures.

FOURTH YEAR

In my fourth year I became more exposed to hospital activities,
both inpatient and outpatient, rotating through the specialties
of medicine, surgery, obstetrics and gynecology, pediatrics, and
psychiatry. I was an integral part of a team made up of an attending physician and senior and junior residents during the short
periods I lived in the hospital. However, I was not yet allowed to
do any procedures such as stitching, invasive diagnostic tests, or
delivering babies. I became long on theory, but the hands-on
practice would have to await my internship after graduation.

I was awarded the Wood Gold Medal for placing first in my
class, the College of Physicians and Surgeons of Quebec Prize for
Medicine and Pathology, and the Robert Forsythe Prize in Surgery in my final year of medical school. I remember my mother's
excitement when a former colleague of my father leaked the news
to her the night before its official release. My fiancée, Andrea,

and I went downtown and waited for the early morning edition of the *Montreal Gazette*, which carried the news. I raised my sights to a career in academic medicine.

I graduated on 28 May 1958, and Andrea and I were married two days later. I was on top of the world.

Andrea and John, wedding day, 30 May 1958

2

Expanding Horizons during Postgraduate Training

Andrea and I returned to Montreal after a two-week honeymoon in Vermont and Cape Cod. We moved into my mother's house – not an ideal situation for newlyweds, but necessary because of our financial situation. I was earning $40 monthly as a married intern, and Andrea contributed $250 monthly as a graduate nurse at the MGH. When we had approached him one year previously with our intention to marry, my future father-in-law had asked how I was going to support his daughter. He was not impressed when I said we would manage on Andrea's salary and live with my mother, but seemed to accept that I was a good long-term risk.

We had a large house to ourselves during our first summer as my mother was away at her country home in Vermont. However, as I worked every second night and every second weekend and was awake most of my time on call, my new wife and I did not have a lot of time together. It was even more difficult for Andrea when my mother returned after Labour Day and she and Andrea were housemates 50 per cent of the time. However, Andrea and I were young and in love and easily managed this lifestyle for two years.

INTERNSHIP AND JUNIOR RESIDENCY AT THE MONTREAL GENERAL HOSPITAL

My first year was a rotation through the major medical specialties then required for medical licensure. I began on the newborn ward at the Montreal Children's Hospital, a harrowing experience for a newly minted doctor with little practical experience. Although my senior residents were very helpful and understanding, the attending staff was less so. I learned to draw blood from an opening in an infant's skull (the anterior fontanelle) and to insert needles into the spinal column in cases of suspected meningitis. It would have been easier to learn these procedures on an adult, but at least my first patients could not complain of my lack of dexterity, and I had no significant complications. I learned my suturing from treating frequent lacerations in the emergency department, and soon I was beginning to feel like a real doctor.

My most frightening experience was being called to the bedside of a blue baby in the middle of the night. The infant had only one lower heart chamber instead of two and in the absence of any possible corrective surgery could not survive long. It is one thing to look after an elderly patient near death with a terminal illness, but quite another to be responsible for a dying one-month old infant. Fortunately a senior resident quickly responded to my panic call and stabilized the patient.

The other rotations during my first year internship were less exciting but still exhausting. Obstetrics and gynecology call was forty-eight hours on and forty-eight off, so I spent most of my first day home sleeping. Delivering babies was particularly rewarding because there was usually a happy outcome. However, before the days of ultrasound, congenital abnormalities were rarely anticipated before delivery. One night I could not deliver the baby's head and called in the staff obstetrician who recognized hydrocephalus (a huge head due to excess water in the ventricles of the brain). He had to crush the baby's skull with forceps to complete the delivery, a sad and unexpected outcome for the young couple who were eagerly anticipating parenthood.

During my surgical rotation I mostly held skin retractors and watched, but Dr Alan Thompson, a very patient senior surgeon, allowed me to do several appendectomies. My wife found me on a high for several days after my first one. The schedule over Christmas or New Year's was seven days on and seven days off. I once went without sleep for nearly forty-eight hours and had to be sent out of an operating room. Fortunately, these ridiculously excessive on-call hours have since been corrected. My medical rotation was slower by comparison, but as that was where my future lay, I found it more intellectually stimulating, despite the fact that many attending staff physicians treated interns as slaves. Dr Douglas Cameron, the physician-in-chief, was demanding and insistent on high standards. He was an excellent teacher and encouraged me towards a path to academic medicine. Psychiatry was interesting, but as it was less hands-on, I did not feel the same degree of accomplishment.

My apprenticeship was completed as I entered my second year of training at the MGH. I had first-year interns under me and was in a position to guide them out of new situations as my seniors had done for me a year before. I was now certain that I wanted to become a cardiologist, but a full four-year training program in Internal Medicine had to come first, as there were not yet certifications in the subspecialties. I spent a month in dermatology under Dr R.R. Forsey, my father's successor as head of the department. He did his best to attract me to his specialty, but I was by then convinced of a cardiology career and also did not want to follow so closely in my father's footsteps and risk spending my professional life being compared with him.

On my first day in dermatology clinic I met Mr Roy, the orderly who organized the patient flow. My father had trained him to give injections and do other minor procedures. He had become a legend – being called "Doctor" by many patients, a designation he did not dispute. One day in the waiting room full of patients he confronted me and said, "You are going to go into dermatology like your father, eh, Dr Burgess?" When I replied that I was headed towards cardiology, he gave me a disdainful look and bellowed, "You're crazy, Dr Burgess! You will make a lot more money in dermatology."

I had about thirty sets of eyes trained on me. I could not think of a suitable reply, but luckily Dr Forsey saved me by calling me to see a patient. He later told me he was not sure Mr Roy's opinion was correct.

I had to make a decision on my future. About halfway through my second year of internship I felt ready to begin training in cardiology and cardiac research. I was finishing nine years at McGill institutions. Andrea also felt we must strike out on our own after two years living with my mother. We both looked forward to going abroad and were considering England. However, this was not the accepted path. Internal medicine trainees were expected to do four years of internal medicine and a year of pathology in their home institution before entering specialty training elsewhere. I felt that recent developments in physiology and biochemistry were replacing pathology as the basic sciences for internal medicine. I had had two intensive years of pathology in medical school.

Dr Cameron, the physician-in-chief, was strongly opposed to my proposed course. He told me I must stay at the MGH and complete the standard training. He would then support me in a bid for cardiology training in the United States or abroad. At this juncture I really missed my father's advice. I turned to my best friend's father, George Ferguson, who was editor-in chief of the *Montreal Star*, the city's afternoon English paper. He had always taken an interest in my career, and in some ways was a second father to me. A former Rhodes scholar, he supported my idea of going to England and suggested I would be a strong candidate for a Nuffield Travelling Fellowship.

Dr Cameron was not pleased that I was charting a course against his advice, and it was risky to challenge him. He told me that the Nuffield Fellowship allotted to McGill for the coming year had already been awarded. I'm not sure what George Ferguson did behind the scenes, but I shortly received a letter from the Nuffield Foundation saying that a second application from McGill would be considered. I applied and was successful. Dr Cameron could not oppose two fellowships from this prestigious foundation for his residents.

I had initially been accepted for training at the London Heart Hospital, but a senior colleague of Dr Cameron's advised me that I would obtain a better research experience in Birmingham. Andrea and I were off to England with the chief's blessing.

TWO YEARS AT THE QUEEN ELIZABETH HOSPITAL, UNIVERSITY OF BIRMINGHAM, ENGLAND

We were set to sail from Montreal to Southampton in July 1960, but because of a strike, were flown to Manchester instead. Andrea was nauseated during the flight and sick to her stomach on the train south to Birmingham. We arrived in a strange city and a different country exhausted and unkempt without a place to stay. Fortunately Dr Geoff Aber, the senior registrar (resident or fellow) on Professor Melville Arnott's unit where I was to train, had been at the MGH the year before. He found us a place to stay and took me to the hospital the next day. A senior registrar in cardiology, Dr Mary Stanley, and her husband, Eric, a professor of medieval history at the university, had an upper flat in their home for rent, and in a few days we moved in. Their friendship provided an important dimension to our next two years.

Andrea's stomach problems continued, and she soon discovered she was a few weeks pregnant. Previously she had contended that morning sickness in pregnancy was psychological, but personal experience changed her view. Our lives were changing rapidly in many ways.

It was another large transition for me beginning life on the ward of the Queen Elizabeth Hospital and in a research laboratory. I was appointed to the position of a middle-grade registrar (equivalent to a third-year resident at McGill). I was responsible for a ward of thirty-five patients, with a house officer below me. I reported to a lecturer (one step below a staff physician). The consultant physician, Dr Peter Harris, made rounds for about two hours twice weekly. The only other formal teaching session was a one-hour Department of Medicine conference each Friday. When I encountered something I was unfamiliar with, such as a heart murmur, I would seek out on my own a more senior person for advice. As I was also a research fellow, I was given a laboratory room in an adjacent building and started on a research project involving lung circulation under Dr John Bishop.

The professorial unit was well staffed with physicians in training. My associates, instead of being mostly former classmates and graduates of other Canadian medical schools, were from all over the world. In addition to Britain, they came from Australia, New Zealand, central and South Africa, India, and Pakistan. Andrea and I were by far the youngest married couple and enjoyed having the bachelors to dinner in our modest three-room flat. Our new friends frequently invited us for dinner, the usual menu being sherry and a "joint" – a leg of lamb. I was on night call only once in ten days, so I had more time at home with my pregnant wife.

The occasional formal dinners were more daunting experiences than our casual dining. We were invited to Nuffield House in London with the other current travelling fellows. They were all older, professors of basic and social sciences from all parts of the Commonwealth, and considerably more worldly-wise than Andrea and I. After dessert our host, the director of the Nuffield Foundation, announced that the ladies would retire to another room for coffee and liqueurs while the men stayed to discuss the weighty affairs of the world over cigars and cognac. Andrea was insulted by being banished in this manner but managed to keep her feelings to herself. We since wondered what would have happened if one of the travelling fellows had been female. As the Nuffield Fellowships were discontinued a few years later, this problem never arose.

In England we adapted to a very different lifestyle than the one we had in Montreal. We had no telephone and depended on our landlord's for emergencies. There was no refrigerator, and so Andrea shopped every day, and milk was delivered to our door. In the absence of central heating, we sat close to the gas fire on cold, damp winter nights. Our heating costs were three to four shillings daily, and we soon learned that a coal-oil heater was more efficient and less expensive. Smog from mostly coal-heated buildings was a severe problem in the industrial Midlands. If it rained, Andrea would have to rewash the laundry that had been hanging outside to dry because it would be covered with a thin layer of coal dust. Smog could also be a driving hazard. One night we decided it would be safest to follow a bus to our destination. Suddenly I realized that visibility was so low that even the bus had stopped at the curb. We turned around and slowly made our way home. The next day one of my colleagues noted that following other vehicles was risky: he had once stopped behind a private car in the owner's driveway.

During our first winter I was asked to drive the professor home from London – he had not used his own car because of a couple of centimetres of snow on the ground. I had bought a Volkswagen for later export to Canada. As we cruised up the motorway, I could see that my passenger was uncomfortable. Finally Professor Arnott looked at me and said, "I say, Burgess, we're right on the road, aren't we?" He found the trip back to Birmingham in my little car a different experience, being so low to the ground compared to his large Rover. When we reached his house, he thanked me for a safe drive, but then said, "I say, Burgess, this is a well-engineered vehicle, but I would never buy a German car." I had not lived in the industrial English Midlands during the 1941 bombing of the factories.

Most of my peers from other parts of the Commonwealth felt that they were coming home to the mother country. Andrea and I did not share this view, being more closely associated with the United States. The first time I entered a post office to buy stamps for letters home and asked the price, I was surprised to receive the answer, "It's the same to all the colonies."

CLINICAL TRAINING AT THE
QUEEN ELIZABETH HOSPITAL

British training programs have been known for generations to emphasize bedside skills rather than technology in arriving at a diagnosis. I was assigned to a thirty-two bed ward for two years. On Friday mornings I often attended a mitral clinic (for disorders of the valve preventing blood from leaking backwards when the left side of the heart pump contracted). Both staff physicians and those in specialty training had access to a large volume and variety of patients unobtainable in North America. This would stand me in good stead during my later Arctic practice when I had to rely on bedside skills with few technological tools to aid me.

Rheumatic fever, a complication of streptococcal throat infections, was still common in the British Midlands. I would not encounter as much valvular heart disease again until my trips to northern Canada. Artificial valves were not yet available in the late 1950s. Mitral stenosis, a narrowing of the mitral valve, could be corrected without open-heart surgery, but there was no repair for other valve conditions. Attempts were made to replace damaged leaflets with Teflon ones, but these always failed soon after surgery. I would watch these patients gradually deteriorate during repeated visits and learned that most could survive years without surgery with few symptoms. Knowledge of the natural history of disease is essential, as surgery can often be delayed.

Implanted pacemakers for electrical malfunctions of the heart were not yet available either. The batteries to power the system were too large to be placed in a body cavity or under the skin. An ingenious device had been made in London to pace the heart of patients whose rates were too slow. This consisted of a wire attached to the right ventricle (the chamber pumping blood to the lungs) leading to an induction coil under the skin of the chest wall. A second coil attached to a battery pack on a belt was placed over it, and the current went to the internal coil through the skin. This was a very effective temporary solution. However, if the two coils became unopposed during dressing, bathing, or exercise, the device no longer paced the heart. The heart rate would suddenly slow, and the patient would collapse. The advent of small mercury batteries led to the totally implantable devices now used.

Many patients with coronary artery disease present as sudden death – a cardiac arrest in the absence of previous symptoms. Closed-chest massage to maintain the circulation until a defibrillator was available when the heart stopped was first described in late 1960 but was not used until 1962.[1] Before then it was necessary to open the patient's chest with a knife and massage the heart internally. This technique only sustained about 25 per cent of the normal blood flow and was rarely successful, especially when the arrest occurred outside of the hospital. Professor Arnott's brother died in 1961 after suffering brain damage when resuscitation was not immediately available.

In the absence of intensive care units, Professor Arnott arranged for acute heart attack patients to be placed inside the entrance to the wards. Medical students were assigned on continuous eight-hour rotations to watch an oscillograph screen by the bedside, a form of slave labour that I doubt would have passed student councils in North America. A scalpel was placed under a napkin on the bedside table. The student would summon a nearby registrar if a heart irregularity occurred. This plan anticipated the advent of coronary care units with sophisticated monitoring equipment by two years, but I do not recall any lives being saved. Artificial heart valves, implantable pacemakers, closed chest massage, and coronary units arrived shortly after my return to Montreal. I was ready for them.

TEACHING

All registrars on the unit were expected to teach medical students. Although I had some experience in bedside and weekly conference teaching, I was nervous when I was assigned to teach a full course in physical diagnosis to a group of ten students. It was a challenge, as North American graduates are not as proficient in these skills as their u.k. counterparts. I bought the appropriate textbook and spent many evenings staying just one session ahead of the class. One problem was adapting to a different accent. When I asked the students how to say a certain word with an English accent, one politely told me, "Sir, you can't speak English with an English accent. It is you who has the accent."

There is nothing like having to teach a subject to improve one's own understanding of the topic. Confidence in small-group and whole-class teaching comes from the knowledge that the lecturer has a better grasp of the subject than the pupils. I often tell aspiring teachers that if they cannot explain a concept clearly to students, they do not understand it well enough themselves. Although some of my undergraduate learning came from small-group sessions, these were not nearly as extensive as those I taught in Birmingham. I became convinced of the value of small groups compared with whole-class didactic lectures.

MY INITIATION INTO CARDIAC RESEARCH

Dr John Bishop was my research supervisor during my two years in Birmingham. Like most British faculty members, he had done a BTA (Been to America) year in Philadelphia and learned a technique for measuring the blood volume of the smallest lung vessels (pulmonary capillaries). He wanted to establish this technique at the Queen Elizabeth Hospital. I was assigned to assemble the equipment. I was very fortunate to embark on research by developing a new technique and applying it to patients rather than becoming part of an already established team and project. This was the best way to begin clinical investigation. I learned later at the Cardiovascular Research Institute in San Francisco and on my return to McGill that many research trainees, and even established investigators, did not understand their tailor-made equipment. They therefore were unaware of its limitations and possible incorrect results.

The technique I learned from John Bishop and the equipment we built from scratch make up the pulmonary diffusing capacity test. It measures the permeability of the membranes of the lung and the volume of the capillaries exposed to gas exchange. The diffusing capacity of the lung can be measured by having a subject, patient or animal, inhale a very small percentage of carbon monoxide, which has a high affinity for hemoglobin in red blood cells. I was anxious to start studying patients, but I first had to get the equipment working.

A small red cylinder of pure carbon monoxide was delivered to my laboratory. I then set up a mercury-filled system to dilute this poisonous gas in air. It was this apparatus that resulted in my first research disaster. One Saturday morning I arrived in my lab to find that a connection had broken. There was one pound of mercury all over the floor. Mercury is not called quicksilver for nothing: I spent the rest of the day chasing the substance with a broom and dustpan, filtering it into a flask, and coaxing it back into my mixing apparatus.

After about three months of assembling equipment and testing the method for accuracy and repeatability on normal people, I was ready to study a disease. John Bishop felt that the diffusing capacity not only measured the passive transfer of oxygen in the lung but also depended on the amount of hemoglobin in its vessels. Patients with polycythemia vera have too much hemoglobin. We would study them before their treatment, when their hemoglobin became normal, and in some cases when they later became anemic.

Unlike most other university medical centres, the Queen Elizabeth Hospital was the only tertiary referral base for nearly eight million people. This enabled us to find sufficient patients with this rare disease. Our hypothesis proved true: the diffusing capacity fell over a period of months as the hemoglobin fell. We developed a formula for correcting this widely used test for varying hemoglobin concentrations and also showed that some of our patients had a reduced diffusing capacity because of blood clots in small vessels – a known complication of the disease. The next step was to present our work at a scientific meeting.

The British Medical Research Society (MRS) met on the last Friday evening of each month in London. A majority of our staff researchers and those in training closed shop at noon on Friday and departed for London to attend the meeting, held at the various London teaching hospitals. One registrar would be left at home to look after our patients. I usually took Andrea with me, and we would stay with friends for the weekend and often attend a play or opera. Professor Arnott once asked me with a smile if I would attend the meetings if they were held in Stoke-on-Trent. I replied that my attendance would not be as regular.

In preparation for my big event, I spent a month analyzing my results and drawing diagrams suitable for projection slides. I rehearsed my allotted ten minutes on the stage numerous times at home with Andrea and finally at weekly research rounds. I learned that if I read from notes, eminent professors in the back row would begin stamping their feet. Fortunately the presentation went well. The back row smiled benignly on the young colonial and asked a few polite questions. The abstract was published in the MRS proceedings. I was on my way to becoming a clinical investigator, but I still had to prepare a manuscript for publication – in a top-rate medical journal, I hoped. John Bishop spent as much time editing my paper as I spent writing it. It was published in 1963 as the lead article in the *Journal of Clinical Investigation*, one of the best American research journals. I had aimed for the top and reached it on my first try.

ANDREA AND I BECOME PARENTS

Our daughter, Willa, was born in May, two months short of our first year in Birmingham. Andrea's water broke before labour began and I took her to the Birmingham maternity hospital early in the morning. A kindly Scottish sister (head nurse) greeted us and immediately recognized young colonials requiring special attention. Like most senior British maternity nurses, she had midwifery training and sized up the situation quickly. A nurse took Andrea off to her room, and I was ushered into Sister's office. "This is going to take some time," she told me. Another nurse then arrived with a plate of eggs, bacon, toast, and coffee, which I ate at Sister's desk. I doubt that I would have received that treatment in Montreal.

Sister's initial prognosis proved correct. The baby's head would not turn, and an emergency Caesarean section was required. Andrea's mother, who had come to be with us for the birth of her first grandchild, was more anxious than we were, but all went well. I went home to our flat and after several hours of negotiation on our landlord's phone, managed to get through to my mother with the news.

We took our firstborn home one week later. Again we adapted to a major lifestyle change. Six weeks later Willa accompanied us on a tour of northern England and Scotland. The next spring the three of us spent four weeks on the continent. Although our mothers did not look kindly on these adventures, Andrea was not going to let a new baby deprive us of the educational experience of travel.

3

Return to North America

After two years away, we returned to Montreal in July 1962. My mother, who had not yet seen her first grandchild, met us at the dock with Andrea's parents. Andrea was six months pregnant, so it was an exciting reunion. We moved into a lower duplex subsidized by my mother. My salary at the Montreal General Hospital had risen to $250 monthly, but my wife was now a full-time mother.

I spent my first year back as a senior resident on a thirty-five bed ward. Research would have to wait for two years, but I enjoyed showing off my new-found clinical skills to junior colleagues and teaching students. The latter activity would gradually play an even larger part in my career than research. Our second daughter, Cindy, arrived in October. Our home life was now full with two young children and my studying during most waking moments for my Royal College Fellowship exams.

I became chief resident in medicine during my second year back. This entailed a fair bit of administration, arranging schedules and weekly rounds, experience that would be valuable when

I later became chief of Cardiology. However, the best part of the year was answering medical consults from all the other departments in the hospital. There were not yet well-developed specialty services, and daily I would see six or more new consultations across a wide range of internal medicine. I had no assigned supervision, but could go to any staff specialist I wanted when I needed help. I now felt like an independent consultant physician. I attached myself to the Cardiology Division under Dr E.A.S. Reid, who had just become chief, but my main role model was Dr Patrick Cronin. He was the first university full-time member of Cardiology and brought basic and clinical research to the MGH. He would become my closest colleague and a dear friend.

ROYAL COLLEGE FELLOWSHIP EXAMS

The Royal College of Physicians and Surgeons of Canada exams were the largest hurdle for any Canadian aspiring to become a medical or surgical specialist. These were a series of three written exams in September, each three hours long, on the practice of medicine, basic science in medicine, and pathology. That year, 1963, was the last in which a separate paper and oral exam in pathology was included. This latter particularly worried me as I had not studied it or looked at specimens or microscopic slides since second-year medical school. I had to pass it, as I had told the physician-in-chief, Dr Douglas Cameron, three years previously I did not need this year of training. Three weeks later Andrea phoned me at the hospital, saying a telegram had arrived inviting me to the oral exams in Toronto during November. Now my wife really became an examination widow.

I felt quite confident after my short and long case oral exams in medicine – in fact I made a clinical diagnosis that the examiners had not considered – but pathology awaited the next day.

33

It was held in the basement of the Banting-Best Institute of the University of Toronto. Candidates were handed specimens that looked at least a hundred years old in formaldehyde sealed in glass jars. The challenge for the microscopic slides was as much to identify the tissue as the actual disease.

The results of the exams that would determine my future were still announced in a barbaric fashion. Candidates were assembled in the foyer of the private patient pavilion of the Toronto General Hospital and they were then called one by one to the front. If the chief examiner shook your hand and invited you next door for sherry, you had passed. If he looked at you without an extended hand, you had failed. I received the handshake and sherry. Afterwards, I ran out to a payphone and called Andrea. When I became chief examiner in Cardiology years later, I handed out the results in sealed envelopes.

CODE 99

The realization that sudden cardiac death due to an irregularity of the heart's rhythm (ventricular fibrillation resulting in a lack of heart muscle contraction) could be reversed by an early electric shock led to the placing of patients at high risk on monitors at the end of the ward in Birmingham. We now needed a rapid response system throughout the MGH. During the spring of 1964, the chief of Cardiology, Dr Stewart Reid, assigned me the task of setting up such a system. The words "Code 99" would be broadcast over the hospital public address system (personal pagers were as yet unknown), together with the location where the cardiac arrest occurred. An arrest team consisting of myself, or a senior medical resident on call, an anesthetist, and a nurse would rush to the scene with a defibrillator to terminate the abnormal rhythm.

The Gazette

WEDNESDAY, JUNE 10, 1944

★ ★

prestolite

THE BATTERY WITH A QUICK
PRESTOLITE LIMITED
1353 Dufferin St., Toronto, Ont.
Also plants in Drummondville,
Quebec, and Calgary, Alberta.

Serving Canadians for 50 Years

Three-Time Heart Arrest Winner Re-Enacts Grim Drama

... The Code 99 rushes the electronic defibrillator machine to his bedside while nurse Gail Tedstone (right) administers intravenous fluids and Dr. Robillard continues the ventilator operation. Dr. Burgess gets ready to deliver an electric shock through two insulated paddles. When nurse Sharon Johnston (left) pushes the button the unconscious patient will visibly "jump" at the shock's impact. If all goes well, his heart will start beating again. If not, death is permanent, not temporary ...

Doctors: "Action Stations!"
And Death Takes A Holiday

... It's a laughing matter now, following a "staged" recreation of the operation. But only days before Mr. Percy came within seconds of losing his life in the same hospital bed. But now he can give his thanks to modern science and joke with his grinning rescuers. The hospital team saved 10 of 17 cardiac arrest victims in the April and May ...

Code 99

I will never forget the first MGH Code 99. It was eleven o'clock at night when the team was called to a single room on one of the medical wards (patients with heart attacks were not yet segregated in coronary care units). The patient was receiving closed chest massage to maintain his circulation. I carried a small red box capable of delivering 400 volts to terminate his ventricular fibrillation. I placed paddles connected to the defibrillator on his chest and in an authoritative manner asked everyone to stand back. I pushed a red button, there was a crash, and all the lights on the ward went out. The hospital outlets were not fused to carry 400 volts. Someone arrived with a flashlight, and I was pleased to find that, although the patient had not survived our first Code 99, at least I had not caused a cardiac arrest amongst any of my fellow health-care professionals.

The fuse problem was remedied the next day throughout the hospital, and subsequent Code 99s were more successful. The first resuscitated patient and I, a student nurse, and attending anesthetist were featured on the front page of the *Montreal Gazette*. My place in the sun was brief, as I prepared to end my clinical training.

CALIFORNIA HERE WE COME

Before leaving Birmingham, Professor Arnott had strongly advised me to take further research training at the best cardiac institution in the world. This was the Cardiovascular Research Institute in San Francisco, directed by Dr Julius H. Comroe Jr. I had applied for and been awarded an R.S. McLaughlin Fellowship, which would provide financial support for two years.

Andrea and I and our two daughters, aged three years and eighteen months, left for San Francisco on 1 July 1964. Andrea was pregnant with our third child. We stopped to say goodbye to my mother and Andrea's parents, who looked anxiously at our overloaded station-wagon. Canada Day was not the best date to start on our journey. We spent about two hours in traffic just getting off the island of Montreal, but had smoother sailing afterwards. We drove for six days, averaging about five hundred miles daily, and spent five nights in campgrounds to save our meagre funds. We started out at dawn, paused briefly for lunch, and stopped at state parks by five P.M. Andrea started dinner on a portable stove while I set up a tent and the girls played nearby.

I had my first experience in American medicine en route. In the middle of Montana we came across an accident. Two young boys had driven their small car into the back of a trailer truck. We were among the first on the scene. Andrea drove the girls to an adjacent roadside restaurant while I assessed the two accident victims. One was dead and the other seriously injured but stable. After the police and ambulances had departed, I was surprised to be told by a bystander that a doctor should not stop for highway accidents for fear of being sued. I replied that, whatever the consequences, I could not drive by an injured person unless medical personnel were already on the scene. I subsequently learned that most states have Good Samaritan laws protecting doctors who provide reasonable care to car accident victims.

We arrived safely in San Francisco. Andrea and the girls went hunting for a small affordable house while I attended introductory sessions at the Cardiovascular Research Institute.

TWO YEARS AT THE CARDIOVASCULAR RESEARCH INSTITUTE (CVRI), SAN FRANCISCO

The senior staff at the CVRI was world famous in cardiac and respiratory research. I had never encountered so much talent in one place. Under the direction of Dr Comroe, they provided a formal research-training program. During the summer all new fellows were given courses in statistics, mathematics, and cardiac and respiratory physiology. The staff members presented their research so that we could decide which program we wished to pursue. There was a journal club every Friday where we learned critical review of the scientific literature, and at Saturday morning sessions attended by all fellows and staff, research in progress was presented.

Dr Comroe was very interested in the careers of his fellows. Every Saturday morning we gave presentations on the culture of our home countries. I gave a talk on "The French Fact in Canada." Our presentations were videotaped and later critiqued by colleagues and staff. It was quite an experience to see oneself lecturing on film. It revealed many mannerisms and other faults that needed correction. This training had a large impact on my future teaching.

RESEARCH AT THE CVRI

Dr Jay Nadel, a senior staff member, was interested in clinical (patient-oriented) research and in my experience with the diffusing capacity technique. I joined his group and, along with his other fellows, published two papers on disorders of the lung circulation. Jay Nadel also involved me in more basic animal research, an area where I had no previous experience. I adapted my diffusing capacity technique to dogs, and we studied the effect of large blood vessel pressures in the lung on the small (capillary) vessel volume. These studies resulted in a paper in the *Journal of Applied Physiology*, which enhanced my bibliography for applying for grants as an independent researcher back at McGill. I also learned the technique of cardiac catheterization (the passage of tubes into the human heart to measure pressure and blood flow) under Dr Elliot Rapaport and studied the effects of drugs on the circulation. I was well prepared for independent research after my two years at the CVRI.

LIFE IN SAN FRANCISCO

As in Birmingham, CVRI research fellows came from all over the world. Andrea and I made many new and lasting friendships, particularly with colleagues who also had young families. Groups of us would meet on Sundays at nearby beaches and redwood forests for picnics. We had no spare money, but all our friends were in the same position so it did not matter. One set of parents would babysit while the others went down to Fisherman's Wharf for dinner or attended the San Francisco Opera on student tickets. Our third daughter, Lynn, was born in October 1964. Our favourite bachelor in Birmingham, Dr Sam Cole, came to the CVRI during my second year. By that time he had married, and the Coles had their first daughter a week after our third. Andrea and Jane Cole became close friends. When we all dispersed, it was very hard to part with our friends, but many friendships lasted a lifetime. Norman and Di Jones from London later moved to McMaster University in Hamilton, Ontario. Our families would frequently visit back and forth, and many years later we would attend the weddings of each other's children.

WE RETURN TO MONTREAL

We returned home at a more leisurely pace than on our trip west two years earlier. We drove up the west coast to Vancouver and across Canada, camping every night for six weeks. Willa and Cindy, now five and three, could hike for fair distances in the national parks, and we took turns carrying Lynn in an early-model backpack. We spent a week in Olympic National Park in Washington and another week in Banff and Jasper Parks in Alberta. I gave lectures at the medical schools in Washington, Edmonton, and Winnipeg for $50 apiece to help pay for the gas. We arrived home at the beginning of August in time for me to take up my duties as a cardiologist at the Montreal General Hospital. At the age of thirty-three years, I was finally able to earn a respectable living for my family.

4

Cardiologist at the Montreal General Hospital and McGill University

I had been awarded a Medical Research Council of Canada Scholarship, which paid my salary and stipulated that I must spend 75 per cent of my time in research. I also had grant support from the Medical Research Council and the Heart Foundation of Quebec for laboratory expenses. I spent August in clinical duties and setting up my laboratory for clinical research. I continued with my diffusing capacity technique, which would last the duration of my research career, and shared a technician and animal laboratory with Pat Cronin, who was in charge of cardiac research. I enjoyed the clinical work and began my own practice from an office in the hospital. I particular enjoyed the teaching on ward rounds and during conferences. Before long I was asked to give lectures in first-year physiology and a a second-year introductory course in clinical medicine.

My research started out well. I presented papers at Canadian and American meetings and published one to two original research articles annually in peer-reviewed journals. I was also enjoying teaching at the bedside. But the most difficult thing for a clinician-scientist is to protect time for research, and this soon became my problem. Pat Cronin and I were the only two of an eight-member division to have university salaries. Our colleagues felt that we were paid to do most of the teaching. I was frequently the only cardiologist in the hospital after the noon-hour and then would be called for consultations and emergencies. I found it increasingly difficult to find time for research. With the exception of Pat Cronin the other staff cardiologists were not very supportive. They had little sympathy for me because of my university salary – the princely sum of $12,000 annually – and my lack of office overhead.

After I had been home for two years, I was offered a very attractive position at the University of California, San Francisco. I looked at this job carefully and saw that it would advance my research and academic career more rapidly than if I stayed at home. Andrea and I now had a big decision to make, with my career on one side and our family life on the other.

Our son, Jay, had just been born in April 1968. There were now six people to consider in any change of career or place of residence. We felt it was a bad time to bring up a young family on the West Coast. If we moved back to San Francisco, our children would be soon exposed to the expanding drug culture. We were also worried that so many of our Californian friends' marriages had already ended in divorce – this seemed to have become the rule rather than the exception in West Coast society. The University of California, San Francisco, would be a much more academically competitive environment, and I would have less time for my family. In addition, we would be away from my aging mother and Andrea's parents and unable to spend summers in Vermont.

41

I turned to Pat Cronin for advice. He advised me to stay at the MGH, even suggesting that I would soon be the leading candidate for chief of Cardiology. We decided to stay in Montreal and at McGill. My research and teaching continued to thrive despite an increasing patient load. Even though the Quiet Revolution in Quebec soon became more violent, we never regretted our decision.

I became cardiologist-in-chief in 1973 and remained in that position until 1994. I was able to attract a strong succession of clinical and research trainees, but my own time for research again declined. Fortunately, the Division of Cardiology prospered in this area as young full-time staff members, whom I had sent to train abroad following a path similar to mine, returned to McGill. Although some subsequently left for other positions, I remain proud to have trained people like Dr Wayne Warnica, now director of Coronary Care at the University of Calgary, and Dr Jean-Lucien Rouleau, who went on to become chief of Cardiology at Sherbrooke, then at the University of Toronto; he is now dean of Medicine at the University of Montreal.

Shortly after my return from California, I was asked to be an oral examiner in Internal Medicine for the Royal College of Physicians and Surgeons of Canada. I found this a very stimulating experience. I met new colleagues from across Canada, saw a variety of interesting patients, and enjoyed the interaction with the candidates. These examining experiences led me to become more involved with the Royal College.

I also began cardiology consulting visits to community hospitals outside of Montreal. These not only increased my clinical experience but also gave me the chance to interact with family physicians on a regular basis. This led to my becoming the first regular consulting cardiologist to the Canadian Arctic.

Both my Royal College work and my outside consulting visits took time. Some of my colleagues resented my days away from the MGH. On my return, I would have to make up night call and other duties. However, these associations greatly enhanced my clinical and academic career. Most of my colleagues at the hospital agreed that they also brought prestige to McGill University and patient referrals to the hospital.

5

Road to the Presidency of the Royal College of Physicians and Surgeons of Canada

My teaching and academic interests led me to increasingly responsible roles in the Royal College of Physicians and Surgeons of Canada. The Royal College was founded in 1929 to grant recognition to all specialties of medicine and surgery in Canada. My father was a charter member. The college not only certifies specialists by examination but is also responsible for the accreditation of university training programs and the maintenance of competence after certification and acts as an advisor to government and other agencies.

I began as an examiner for medicine in the specialty of obstetrics and gynecology shortly after my return from San Francisco. I then became an examiner in internal medicine and later a member, then chairman, of the multiple choice test committee in internal medicine. My children remember my sitting in a lounge chair on the dock of our country home, proofreading questions. The computer printouts were about three inches thick and there were hundreds of possible questions. I became an examiner in cardiology for five years and was chief examiner for a final two years. During my training days there was no Royal College certification in cardiology; I was always careful not to admit to candidates that a non-certified cardiologist was questioning them.

I was a member of the Committee on Accreditation for six years and chaired survey teams at five different medical schools. This was a very valuable experience as it gave me an insight into the pedagogical workings of different institutions. I was made chairman of the Examination Committee and served in this role for six years. Pat Cronin was a member of council – the governing body – of the Royal College. He had to resign this position when he became dean of Medicine of McGill University, and I was nominated to replace him. I became vice-president in 1987, president-elect in 1988, and president from 1990 to 1992. This was a great honour. I met the presidents of other colleges around the world when they attended our annual meeting. Andrea accompanied me when I was given honorary fellowships in the Royal College of Physicians (London), the Royal College of Physicians of Edinburgh, the Royal Australasian College of Physicians, and the College of Physicians of South Africa and when I was made a Master of the American College of Physicians. My presidency greatly expanded the number of our friends around the world.

The Royal College headquarters ran out of space during my presidency, and new accommodation had to be found. I made many trips to Ottawa negotiating with real-estate agents, politicians, and the chairman of the National Capital Commission. The executive director of the college, Dr Gilles Hurteau, carefully guided me through these unaccustomed encounters. On day while driving along the Rideau Canal, he looked at me and said, "How would you like to have that building for our new headquarters?" It was the Monastery of the Sister Adorers of the Precious Blood, a magnifi-

Royal College Council, 1992, author front row centre

cent structure, and it was for sale as the number of cloistered sisters had dwindled. It was a magnificent structure and I was immediately sold on the idea.

The monastery had been bought by real-estate developers who realized that the National Capital Commission would be unlikely to approve its sale except to an organization like our college. The sale price was $6 million, and the necessary renovations were estimated at another $6 million. My committee on finance was opposed to this expenditure, but I was determined to acquire this prestigious heritage building for the Royal College. When the proposal was brought before the council, I chaired the longest and most difficult meeting of my career. It lasted over four hours, but ultimately the motion to buy the monastery passed. Even the three members of council who voted against it later agreed that it had been the right decision. The greatest and final moment of my presidency of the Royal College was officially opening our new headquarters in September 1992.

6

Doctor to the North

When I became director of the Division of Cardiology at MGH in 1973, spending four weeks of the year in the Far North treating heart disease among the Inuit was not my first priority. I therefore remember well the day that the physician-in-chief, Dr Douglas G. Cameron, called me to his office and told me I was the consulting cardiologist to the McGill Baffin Project. There was no discussion.

For the next twenty-five years, I would be the heart doctor for the Baffin Region, later renamed Nunavut ("our land"), Canada's newest territory, established in 1999. As a result of this experience I became the cardiologist to northern Quebec above the 55th parallel – later renamed Nunavik – from 1992 until 2003. The McGill Baffin Project was a contract between the Baffin Regional Health Board and McGill University. It was terminated in 1998 and transferred to the University of Ottawa. The northern Quebec arrangement was a less formal one between the hospitals in Puvirnituk and Kuujjuak and me. It lasted until my retirement from active practice at the end of 2003.

My responsibilities as cardiologist for Nunavut and Nunavik required one-week visits twice yearly to both regions, including visits to the larger nursing stations. During my visits I saw thirty or more patients daily, and between visits I handled several telephone and fax consultations weekly from local family physicians. I saw many changes in disease patterns and delivery of cardiac care over the course of three decades. The infectious disease burden – particularly tuberculosis and viral epidemics – decreased. The lessened risk of streptococcal throat infections spreading through families resulted in a reduced incidence of rheumatic valvular heart disease. While the incidence of inherited types of heart disease has remained stable, the changes in Inuit lifestyle as the people adopt southerners' habits have led to the appearance of coronary heart disease, hypertension, and stroke.

FIRST VISIT TO THE NORTH

It was mid-January 1973 when the jet descended through a gathering blizzard to land in Frobisher Bay – renamed Iqaluit ("a school of fish") in January 1987 and now the capital of Nunavut, with a population of 6,184 in the 2006 census. (The whole of Nunavut – two-thirds of the Canadian Arctic – has a population of nearly 30,000, 85 per cent Inuit.) The captain announced that we would be the last plane in or out for the next twenty-four hours because of the storm. Frobisher Bay had one of the longest runways in the world, built by the United States in 1942 as a transport stop for military supplies to Europe and a holdover from the Cold War of the late 1940s and early '50s when U.S. Strategic Air Command kept nearly 25 per cent of its B52s airborne at all times in case of an unexpected attack.

48

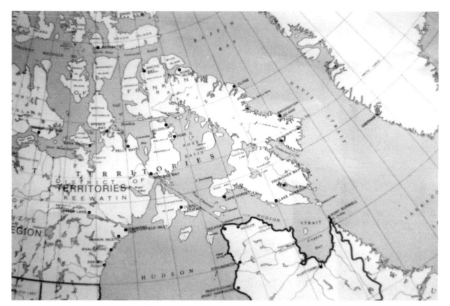

Map of nursing stations in Nunavut and Nunavik, 1975

Arriving in Frobisher Bay (now Iqaluit); high-rise apartment building in centre, power generating station at top left

I was excited but a little nervous as we bounced about, coming in over the frozen bay. The airport had all the facilities for an instrument landing so the poor visibility didn't cause a problem. This, however, was not the case with many of my future flights into smaller settlements by Twin Otter, the famous northern workhorse plane.

After struggling across a frozen runway in the wind, blowing snow, and -25 degree Celsius temperature, I was amazed to find the large single room in the terminus crowded with Inuit of all ages – babies in *amautis* (the hooded parkas still widely used by mothers for carrying their young), children running about, parents and grandparents. The arrival of a plane was a big event. It was customary for whole families to come to the airport to greet a returning relative or friend. Younger Inuit would make the rounds to shake hands and exchange smiling greetings with their seated elders. It was a scene I would encounter over and over again during the next thirty years. I felt confused and lost in the swirl of noisy humanity, until the voice of the hospital driver directed me to his van and drove me to the Frobisher Inn hotel.

The next day was clear, windy, and very cold. As I walked the half-kilometre across a frozen riverbed to the hospital, a feeling of constriction suddenly seized me in my chest, accompanied by shortness of breath. My first reaction was panic over the possibility that I was having a heart attack at the tender age of forty years. Had I been in Montreal, I might have sat on the curb and waited for help, but that was not an option here. I struggled on to the hospital, thinking I would cry for help on getting in the door. However, as soon as I entered the warm reception area, my symptoms quickly abated. I then realized that I had experienced cold-induced bronchospasm (asthma) – a well-known medical phenomenon. From then until this day I use an inhaler before venturing outdoors when the temperature is below 20 degrees Celsius. My first twenty-four hours in the Arctic had been filled with several unforgettable experiences.

It would have been more interesting to time my Arctic visits with the summers when the temperatures vary between the freezing point at night and 5 to 10 degrees Celsius during the days and the sun is up most of the night. There would also have been more time for some local sightseeing and taking wildlife pictures. However, the sea ice is out of the bays for only six to eight weeks of the year. Summer is the time for whole families to move out on the land for hunting and fishing, a return to their historic way of life. My patients would not be available unless they were seriously ill, and I therefore confined my trips to late fall, winter, or early spring.

COMMUNICATING WITH MY PATIENTS
THROUGH INTERPRETERS

Since graduating from medical school, I had been accustomed to talking with my patients in either English or French. I had only occasionally required an interpreter, for Chinese or other languages. In the Arctic I had to learn to work through an interpreter for nearly all my patients. This not only slowed me down – during most days I had to see thirty or more patients at fifteen-minute intervals – but also decreased the degree of empathy possible with my patients. In Nunavut (Baffin), the interpreters would translate from Inuktitut to English, while in Nunavik (northern Quebec), it would be Inuktitut to French.

As the years went by, however, I found that most Inuit under the age of thirty could speak English, which greatly increased my rapport. I also learned that I could communicate with young children by facial expression – an upward glance of the eyes accompanied by a high-pitched sound meant yes, while a downward

Mina, one of my interpreters, and Hershie, head nurse of outpatient department at Baffin Regional Hospital

glance with a low-pitched exclamation meant no. The adults generally expressed little emotion and would rarely thank me.

The head nurse in the outpatient department of Baffin Regional Hospital, Hershie Weinberg, was originally from the Philippines. She had become quite fluent in Inuktitut and was invaluable in organizing my clinics and interpreting for me in Iqaluit and during my settlement visits. Her husband worked for the company providing power for Iqaluit. Hershie and Bob always invited me for dinner during my northern visits and taught me a great deal about Inuit art and culture. Like many couples working for years in the North, they used their accumulated savings to retire in the South – in their case, Mexico.

The Inuit are a stoic people and accept illness or disability with little complaint. I sometimes wondered if they resented me because I represented a culture that exploited theirs and which was responsible for the disease I was trying to improve. However, when I saw a patient back in the North after a procedure in Montreal that had been beneficial, I was usually greeted with a large smile of recognition and the impression that I would be welcome on my next visit.

Despite their restrained approach to their own illness, I found the Inuit to be very demonstrative in their grief over the death of a family member. Once while travelling from Iqaluit to Pangnirtung, a settlement of about thirteen hundred people just south of the Arctic Circle, I was disturbed by the continuous wailing of two women in the back of the small aircraft during the entire hour-long flight. I learned from the cabin attendant that the mother and sister had just lost a young boy to meningitis. The child's body was being brought home for burial.

PATIENT DRESS

My middle-aged and older patients arrived in traditional home-made fur-lined boots and embroidered parkas. Young mothers brought their babies in colourfully embroidered white *amautis* with their large hoods for the infant. I quickly learned how to assist in getting the little one in and out, as the mother was not always able to do this on her own. Young adults and adolescents showed the effect of southern advertising, usually turning up in jeans and running shoes. I never did figure out how they kept their feet from freezing, although I noticed that on small, unheated aircraft they would take off their shoes and tuck their feet under their backsides. In my clinics the men would always throw their outer clothing on the floor beside the examining table. I would pick it up and hang it over a chair so I would not have to stand on it while examining them. I never did ask if they followed this same custom at home and whether their wives picked up after them.

TRAVEL AND ACCOMMODATION

Large jets flew into Iqaluit and Kuujjuak, so arrival and departure were mostly predictable. Travel to the smaller settlements in Twin Otters could be more exciting, especially on the Hudson Bay coast where the airports were usually on elevated ground and invariably windswept. Salluit at the top of Hudson Bay is the second most northern settlement in Quebec. Arriving and departing there was often a fifty-fifty proposition due to sudden blizzards. On several occasions I was stuck for two to three days in a small apartment without radio or television. I learned to bring sufficient reading material for such eventualities. Even getting to the local store to buy food could be a real problem during severe blizzards causing white-outs.

In Iqaluit I stayed in a modern hotel with all the southern amenities, a good dining room, and cable television. The only

U.S. air force base in Frobisher Bay, now demolished

problem was that the town's most popular bar was on the ground floor, and I soon learned to request a room at the other end of the second floor. In the smaller Nunavut settlements I stayed at locally run hotels. Depending on the demand, I often had to share a double room with strangers (invariably men). I usually got along well with my roommates and despite occasional disagreements over television program selection, learned a lot about Inuit history and culture from these encounters.

Hershie accompanied me to the settlements. On one occasion she moved to the nursing station when her roommate invited a male visitor to their room at a late hour. In Puvirnituk and Kuujjuak there were comfortable suites near the hospital for visitors and meals at the hospital. In Inukjuak and Salluit I stayed in cooperative hotels run by the local Inuit Association. Here I would buy my own food and cook in the shared kitchen. This was a satisfactory arrangement except when my arrival was late and the local store had closed. I once arrived in Salluit around 11:00 P.M. to find nobody at the airport to greet me. I managed to hitch a ride down to the nursing station in the back of a pickup truck, together with several amused children. I had to wake the nurse on call to find me accommodation for the night. Fortunately this was the only time in thirty years that my visit was unexpected.

My most interesting times were when I stayed in cooperative small hotels and occasionally in local Inuit homes. In the co-ops I was able to eat and meet with experienced Arctic travellers, usually social workers and teachers, sometimes Inuit, when I could spend time discussing and learning past Inuit history and gain suggestions for the future from different perspectives. I particularly remember staying in the Salluit home of the school headmistress, an Inuk with a Master's degree from McGill University. When I arrived back from a long day in the nursing station, there was always a delicious dinner heating on the stove and the opportunity to talk with her and others visitors. I learned more about Inuit culture during these occasions than from reading books.

INUIT ART

The Inuit art in the living room of my house in Montreal is testament to my many trips to the Arctic. I acquired mostly smaller carvings, as the larger ones had become very expensive, and jewellery for my wife and daughters. Word would get around that the doctor from the South had arrived, and I would be approached to buy carvings, jewellery, or clothing at the hospital or frequently in the hotel dining room. During one of my first visits to Iqaluit I was shown a very nice looking small soapstone. I asked the price, and the young woman replied, "Forty." I reached into my wallet for $40, but she shook her head and said no. When further bargaining did not resolve the problem, I called in my interpreter. After a brief discussion she laughed and said, "She does not mean $40, Dr Burgess. She means forty ounces."

The young woman was interested in trading the carving for liquor, not cash – the government liquor outlet in Iqaluit had been closed, and alcohol was only available in hotel bars. I did not have alcohol in my back pocket, so the deal was off. In general I was reluctant to buy articles from individuals, as one could never be certain of their authenticity or origin. Most settlements had co-op art stores where the price was set and the artist certified.

My favourite dealer was Fred Coman in Iqaluit. He ran the moving company that serviced most of Baffin and had a large back room with a wide variety of artwork. He had hunted with the Inuit in his younger days and directed his operations from a large chair behind his front room desk under rifles and sealskins hanging on the wall. It was apparent that many Inuit carvers preferred to trade with this great white hunter than with local arts

Three of my patients and their mothers in Puvirnituk

Modern art gallery in Pangnirtung: Hershie and manager hold a watercolour by an Inuit artist.

and craft dealers. Fred was a well-known and generous benefactor in the community and always offered me discounts. He later became my patient, so I was able to repay him in a small way.

I learned that specific communities had different wares. Cape Dorset (population 1,236 in the 2006 census, 92 per cent Inuit) – widely recognized as the Inuit art capital of the world – is renowned for its soapstone, Broughton Island (population about 475, and 95 per cent Inuit) for sealskin articles, and Pangnirtung (population 1,325, and 92 per cent Inuit) for prints and weaving. I never came home from a trip to the Arctic empty handed. In addition to carvings, toques and earrings were favourite purchases. When wearing the toques, my four children often found that the distinctive Inuit patterns identified their headgear as coming from the Arctic.

7

History of the Eastern Canadian Inuit

One of my early patients had cardiac surgery to repair an atrial septal defect, a problem with communication between the two upper chambers of the heart. He developed a three-centimetre wide postoperative scar down the front of his chest known as a keloid. While examining him with a Chinese-Canadian physician in Iqaluit, I remarked that I had only seen such keloids in black people. She told me that people of Asian descent are also predisposed to the development of such prominent scars. I recall this as further evidence that the Inuit are descended from East Asian people – probably Mongolian – who emigrated to Alaska and the Canadian Arctic across the Bering Straits before the continents were separated by melting ice.

INUIT VERSUS ESKIMO

Early Inuit were referred to worldwide as Esquimo. An enduring myth is that this name was an Algonquin designation meaning

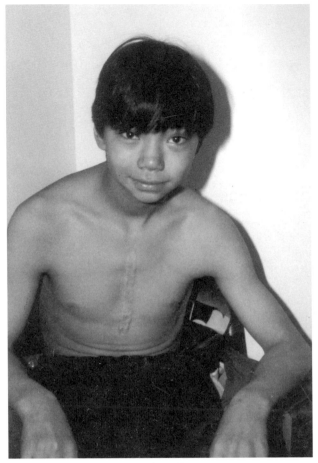

Young Inuit boy with large scar (keloid) suggesting East
Asian origin

"eater of raw meat." However, the evidence for this origin is
sparse. Early European explorers learned the word "Esquimauw"
from the Montagnais Indians, but the derivation is not clear.
Samuel de Champlain believed it to originate from the Inuit
people themselves, writing, "There is an Indian tribe inhabiting
this territory who call themselves Eskimos."[2] Whatever the origin

of the widely used term Eskimo, Inuit people were not Indians, and certainly they did not appreciate being tagged with what they saw as a derogatory term.

The word Inuit means "the people." Small nomadic tribes thought they were the only people on earth until they encountered European explorers and whalers. In 1997, Canadian Inuit delegates at the Inuit Circumpolar Conference officially adopted the term Inuit as the name for all those previously referred to as Eskimos, although properly it describes the aboriginal people of the central Canadian Arctic. The term Eskimo is still used in Alaska and Siberia. Greenland Inuit often refer to themselves as Kaladlit or Greenlanders. An Inuk is an individual of Inuit descent, two are referred to as Innuk, and three or more are Inuit.

INUKTITUT

In the early history of humankind, most new languages were borrowed and modified from the languages of neighbouring societies.[3] Early Inuit had no neighbours to emulate. Their language, called Inuktitut, was unwritten; tribal elders passed down information through generations by stories, which often became mixed with myths and legends. European explorers had little knowledge of Inuktitut and had to rely on interpreters. Information was often embellished depending on the whim of the interpreter and whether he considered the questions asked to be impertinent.

THE FIRST ARCTIC PEOPLES

The peak of the world's last major ice age occurred about 20,000 years ago and was followed by a gradual warming trend in the Canadian Arctic. Archeological evidence indicates that at least six thousand years ago the first humans entered the western Arctic, probably from Siberia across the Bering Strait, either by boat or by walking across the shifting sea ice. Caribou-hunting nomads, they followed the herds north each spring and then retreated south. By around 4000 BCE (Before Common Era) this Paleo-Arctic culture had been succeeded by the Arctic Small Tool Tradition (ASTt) people, probably also from Siberia. The ASTt designation referred to their use of small stone implements for household and hunting use. This group, known also as the Denbigh people, eventually migrated from the Cape Denbigh area in Alaska east-ward across the Arctic and as far as Greenland.

After 1000 BCE, a more advanced culture began to flourish in the Cape Dorset region in the southwest corner of Baffin Is-land. The Dorset people, referred to as Tunit by modern-day Inuit, had more sophisticated tools and hunting weapons and cooking utensils made from ivory and antler tusks. They lived in small groups in dugout dwellings, had sleds for travel, but no dogs or dogsleds. They did not use bows and arrows and did not hunt whales.[4] The Tunit eventually spread across the whole of the Canadian Arctic. They lasted in the Foxe Basin and Hudson Strait until about 1000 CE, but then virtually disappeared. Inuit oral history, confirmed by modern carbon dating and DNA evi-dence, suggests that these people pre-existed modern-day Inuit in the Arctic but were not direct ancestors.

EUROPEAN INVADERS

The first Europeans to visit Baffin came originally from Norway, moving to Iceland during the late 800s and then to Greenland just before 1000 CE. Norse peoples may have traded with the Tunit, representing the first white-aboriginal interaction in the New World. Between 1000 and 1350 they visited the eastern coast of North America, moving as far south as Labrador and Newfoundland. They could herd caribou (called reindeer in Norway) and undertook some agriculture, but Greenland and the frozen Canadian Arctic were not suitable for agriculture or animal domestication.

A twelfth century Norse text refers to the early Inuit as "skraelings" (wretches, inferior beings): "Beyond Greenland, still farther to the north, hunters have come across people of small stature who are called Skraelings. When they are struck with a weapon their wounds turn white and they do not bleed, but if they are killed they bleed almost endlessly. They do not know the use of iron, but employ walrus tusks as missiles and sharpened stones in place of knives."[5]

The Inuit, however, were far superior in the techniques of northern survival. The Norse lasted for 450 years in Greenland but could not survive the beginnings of the Little Ice Age. Those who did not starve or freeze to death retreated to Iceland or Norway, and the Inuit replaced them in the Arctic.[6]

SURVIVAL OF THE INUIT

How did the Inuit become the only people to survive over many centuries in the Arctic? Some anatomical features may have evolved to improve their survival on the cold steppes of Mongolia. Smaller nasal passages allowed less cold air entry into their lungs, while their shorter arms and legs and smaller hands and feet reduced heat loss. However, these physical advantages were probably of minor benefit. The real secret of the Inuit survival was their ability to adapt culturally to a cold, forbidding climate. They learned to make warm clothes from sealskin, still the best outerwear for frigid temperatures. They made snow houses, a superior form of winter housing, and kept warm with oil lamps fuelled by animal fat.

Their techniques of far-north hunting remain unsurpassed. They developed the kayak, a double-pointed, single-man craft covered completely with stretched animal skin – the best vehicle

Traditional hunting by dog team

ever made for northern sea harpooning, and one of the forerun-
ners of the modern canoe. No other primitive society in the
world was more innovative in adapting to its environment.

By this point the Tunit had largely been overtaken by a western Inuit group called Thule. Around 1000 CE this group began
to occupy coastal areas across the Arctic. Oral Inuit histories and
legends talk of battles and displacement of the Tunit.

As the weather warmed and whales and other sea life moved
north, the Thule people followed. In the shallower coastal waters
of the east, they found whales and walruses less numerous and
switched their hunting to caribou, seal, and fish. These Inuit became a more nomadic people, living in smaller groups rather
than larger settlements. Their dog sleds, kayaks, and larger umiaks (similar in construction to kayaks but capable of carrying several people) enabled them to cover large hunting areas. They
moved frequently in good times and bad. Hunters made little at-

Polar bear skin drying on porch

tempt to limit their kills. When caribou migrations became un-
predictable and whaling decreased after 1500 CE,[7] the start of
the so-called Little Ice Age, Inuit began moving south to northern Quebec and Labrador.

PERSISTENCE OF THE INUIT PRIMITIVE
WAY OF LIFE

In the history of humankind, hunters and gatherers like the
Inuit only advanced socially and technologically when they became able to grow food and domesticate animals as both beasts
of burden and part of the food supply. In this way a society could
support larger tribes with specialists for developing advanced
technologies such as writing and tools. The Inuit could not grow
food in the Arctic's climate. They could not borrow new knowledge and technologies from neighbours; distances were too vast

65

and climactic conditions too severe for European invaders to move north after colonizing the southern part of North America. Even twentieth-century European explorers reported encountering small tribes who had never seen white people and rarely other Inuit. The Inuit therefore remained nomadic bands. The bands were small, as women could only carry so much with a child on their back as they moved. Larger tribes with more permanent settlements required the arrival of the British.

Martin Frobisher recorded the British contact with the Inuit in 1576 when he entered the bay now named for him in search of the Northwest Passage. He and his men initially thought they were on an Asiatic shore.[8] On returning to England following his first voyage, Frobisher presented an Inuit hostage as evidence that he had come close to reaching the Orient. The man died shortly thereafter, apparently from an infection acquired aboard ship.

One of Frobisher's men likened the Inuit to the Tartars of Mongolia: "They bee like to Tartars, with long blacke haire, broad faces, and flat noses, and tawnie in color, wearing Seal skinnes, and so doe the women, not differing in the fashion, but the women are marked in the face with blewe streekes downe the cheeks, and round about the eyes."[9] This description gave rise to the speculation that the Inuit originally escaped from warring tribes northward to eastern Siberia and then across the Bering Strait to Alaska.

Most early encounters between Frobisher's men and the Inuit were unfriendly, with hostage-taking and killings on both sides. Frobisher was stabbed in the buttock by an arrow during a minor skirmish, gaining the distinction of being the first known white man to be wounded by an Inuk. Such hostile episodes with visiting white travellers continued, as the Inuit were uncertain whether fighting or friendly trade was more likely to allow them to maintain their territory and preserve their diminishing food supply.

Inuit hunter skinning a seal

Dwindling resources with cooling weather was also the reason for battles between Inuit and Cree Indians of northern Quebec during the 1600s. A second era of cooling during the Little Ice Age lasted until the mid-1800s.

After the 1850s both British and American whalers began wintering around Cumberland Sound and the south of Baffin-Hudson Strait. This increasing contact with Europeans would change the traditional Inuit way of life forever. Many became employees of the whalers, who gave them rifles, ammunition, and food in exchange for working on the whale hunts. The rifle allowed the Inuit to shoot caribou without stalking them at close range, and also to hunt seals on ice floes in the summer, thereby increasing their kill. However, it also meant they had to live near-by the whalers to replenish their ammunition supply. Instead of being constantly on the move, some Inuit began to maintain year-round settlements. They traded at Hudson Bay Company

Seals stored for winter in snow

stores where they obtained food and shelter during times of scarce resources.

The Inuit began to see the white whalers and their outposts as insurance against times of starvation. As they became more dependent on the white invaders, they were less likely to endure the hard life of subsisting on hunting and fishing with resulting frequent periods of starvation. Increasingly they were employed by the whalers – the men as helpers on the whaling vessels, the women as seamstresses – and traded seal blubber for provisions such as food and metal items, particularly knives and needles. The British government, through the whaling captains, provided resource security in times of need and also medical care.

This interaction had lasting effects on Inuit family and social life. Alcohol was introduced into the settlements, and inter-breeding became common. The sailors brought infectious diseases, both sexually transmitted and respiratory, for which the Inuit had no immunity. Hygiene suffered when the Inuit no longer frequently moved from one clean snow house to another but remained in one dwelling. Sedentary settlement life and cramped living quarters encouraged the spread of disease. Families were disrupted as men accompanied the whalers and women stayed home, looking after the children. Mothers became more and more occupied in the preparation of clothing for sale and for their own use. Material possessions increased, especially the ownership of larger sea-going craft; whaleboats given by the whalers in return for services replaced the skin-covered umiaks. Language gradually changed with the introduction of English words.

The incidence of disease increased the more the Inuit adopted the European's lifestyle. An early patient of mine, a respected Inuit elder in Iqaluit, told me that the white man had brought the diseases that I was trying cure. He said, "When we became dependent on your rifle and ammunition, our way of life changed forever. Before you came our food was our medicine. Your food is not good for us."

WHITE MISSIONARIES, POLICE, AND TRADERS TAKE OVER

In 1897 an official Canadian expedition visited Baffin Island and claimed Canadian sovereignty over all the eastern Arctic islands. The Hudson Bay Company established its first Baffin trading post in 1911. These posts soon spread to all eastern Arctic settlements. The traditional Inuit camp life in settlements scattered throughout the Arctic, trappers and hunters providing furs to the Hudson Bay Company, began to disappear, although in the short summers families continued to go out on the land hunting and fishing. The Canadian Inuit, unlike their counterparts in the Soviet Arctic, Alaska, and Greenland, had little say in their governance and became bystanders as a distant Canadian government decided their lives. Unlike other ancient societies that perished because of their abuse of natural resources, the Inuit did not determine their furture by their own acts. The traders, RCMP, and missionaries soon ruled them.

The Hudson Bay Company in 1931 published *The Eskimo Book of Knowledge*, printed in both English and Inuktitut. It was written to improve relationships between the white man and Inuit fur traders, but its writing shows a lack of understanding of Inuit culture. The book emphasized the wish of the king and Great Britain to have the Inuit people share in the advancement of the British Empire. Its thrust was to benefit the white man's side of the fur trade by keeping Inuit hunters healthy. It stated:

The whalers came to your country; the Men of God came and the Traders of the Company came. They altered the conditions of your lives. The bows and arrows which your fathers used, you have discarded for rifles: the kayak and umiak which your fathers used, many of you have discarded for the wooden boats with engines: the rich seal meat [protective against heart disease] and deer meat which were the life blood of all your people, some of you have discarded for White Man's flour.

It was the same way with the officers of the government and with the officers of the company who could not tell at first whether your people derive good or evil from the use of the things the White Man brought to your country.

When you first see a hunter very far away on the ice with his dogs, it is some time before you can tell for certain in which direction he is moving. It was the same way with the officers of the government and with the officers of the Company who could not tell at first whether your people derived good or evil from the use of things which the White Men brought to your country.[10]

The text goes on to excuse actions of the invaders and even suggests many of the ill effects of contact may have been the fault of the Inuit themselves:

> In those days also White Men knew not of the things which are likely to happen when a people such as yourselves suddenly begins to use the things which White Men gradually learned to use over a great period of time.
>
> Take heed to what is written here, all you men and women of the North. Your people have not derived good from the use which you have made of the White Men's things. The things which have been brought to you are good things in themselves, but you have misused some of these things, so that to-day you are a feebler people than in the old days when your fathers did not know the White Men. Your sons are less hardy, your wives bring forth fewer children. Here shall you learn how you have brought this weakness about. There is sickness among some of you. Here you shall learn how you have brought this weakness about.[11]

I wonder how many Inuit were able to read this publication in the early 1930s and what their reaction might have been. The writer lectures them as if they were an ignorant and naughty group of children. It is very revealing of the "white men's" impact on the Inuit and the writer's assessment of responsibility for it. The text makes no apology and does not suggest any necessary change for future governance. The Canadian government in the 1947 published a similar treatise, the *Book of Wisdom for Eskimo*.[12] It also gave junior-school type advice on hygiene and health clearly showing a paternalistic attitude towards the Inuit.

Later Canadian governments treated the Inuit in a similar manner. Rather than considered a distinct society within Canada, they were looked upon as a primitive group needing protection from more developed cultures. The forced move of a group of thirty families from their homes in Inukjuak on the Hudson Bay coast to Grise Fiord in the high Arctic was supposedly to improve their diminishing food supply. In truth, it was based on the need to establish Canadian sovereignty in the North, and particularly over a Northwest Passage shipping route. The perception that a sub-polar group of people could easily adapt their way of life to the most northern permanent settlement in the world created a disaster. Several of my patients in Inukjuak remembered living in Grise Fiord as young children. They had no daylight for several months of the year, and their parents were unable to provide food for the family by hunting and fishing. It was no place for anyone to live year round and certainly not suitable for bringing up children. Many of the displaced people moved back to their northern Quebec home in Nunavik as soon as they regained control of their lives.

After the Second World War, the Cold War between the United States and the Soviet Union resulted in the military development of the North. The u.s. Air Force created instant settlements in the North. Thousands of white men and their machines built military bases and airfields. Inuit men were hired as labourers and hunted only in their spare time. Frobisher Bay became the centre of the eastern Arctic following construction of the Distant Early Warning (DEW) line. The long airstrip became littered with empty oil drums, which would never decay and later had to be removed as part of an extensive cleanup.

The development of a lead-zinc mine at Nanisivik, near the coastal town of Arctic Bay, showed a similar lack of thought for the environment. Its cleanup following the dwindling of commercially viable mineral resources is finally getting underway at great expense, more to the taxpayer than the mining company.

Postwar development of the Arctic increased the ease of travel from the South and between Arctic settlements. It provided easier access to health care and education. But it also disrupted Inuit family life, as children were sent away from their traditional camps to live in hostels from where they could have daily schooling. After 1960 extensive housing was constructed in all settlements for parents following their children.

As the Inuit saw their way of life increasingly under the control of faraway bureaucrats in Ottawa and Yellowknife, they began to demand more from land agreements with the federal and Quebec governments and the establishment of more self-government in a new territory to be called Nunavut. The latter came into existence in 1999. As the Inuit make up over 80 per cent of the population, a new form of self-government was inevitable.

One advantage the Canadian Inuit have over other indigenous cultures that collapsed once their natural resources were destroyed is that the Canadian government has accepted some responsibility for their plight and recognized the need to make long-term restitution for earlier mistakes.

Europeans inadvertently brought infectious disease, which wiped out whole tribes. These epidemics are now largely controlled by the development of hospitals and modern medical practices, but they have been replaced by the degenerative diseases, especially coronary artery disease, brought on by the white man's lifestyle. Modern housing and life in settlements have changed family values and caused psychological difficulties. When Inuit men began to work for whalers' wages, and a century later were employed in airbase and mining construction, they no longer had time to hunt for food and clothing. The women no longer had hides to make clothes and bought these in stores. Food for families was purchased instead of hunted, with the resulting increase in junk food, particularly sugars. Although starvation was no longer a problem, the altered diet brought new health problems.

8

History of Eastern Canadian Inuit Health Care

On one of my early visits to the North, I was about to leave for the airport when a Canadian soldier stopped me in the hospital hallway. "You've got to help me, Doc," he whispered. "I've just woken up with an Eskimo woman in my bed." He clearly felt he had almost certainly been exposed to a sexually transmitted disease and wanted some sort of pill to prevent a future problem. I resisted the temptation to tell him that his female companion was probably at as high or higher risk than himself and instead found a family physician who was competent to deal with the problem.

The soldier had it wrong. It was the white man who brought infectious diseases to the Inuit, often in epidemic form, wiping out whole tribes who had no previous experience of and therefore no acquired resistance to the virus or bacteria. It is often said that before European contact, the Inuit were strong and healthy. They had no infectious diseases – notably absent were influenza, measles, smallpox, whooping cough, and tuberculosis. They were not in the habit of inhaling cigarette smoke. Women wore down their teeth working animal hides into clothing, but they did not rot their teeth eating candy. Babies who survived grew up healthy. The hunting and fishing way of life provided plenty of exercise, and obesity was unknown.

In the nineteenth century before white settlement came to the Canadian Arctic, it is estimated that there was a population of 18,000 Inuit. By the early 1950s, epidemics – mostly viral – had reduced this number by two-thirds to about 6,000.[13] The Inuit were no longer strong and healthy.

Early traders introduced alcohol. When I first went to Iqaluit, there was a government liquor store, and the easy availability of spirits resulted in widespread domestic violence and frequent snowmobile accidents. The closure of this outlet significantly reduced these problems – it is much more expensive to get drunk buying alcohol and beer in a bar or club. In some settlements such as Pangnirtung, alcohol is now prohibited and can only be brought in by special permit. I once arrived in Pangnirtung to find two RCMP constables standing at the bottom of the stairs of the aircraft. I was nervous as I had two bottles of wine for the nursing station staff. Fortunately the Mounties were not interested in me; they took two young women into custody and thoroughly searched the plane, obviously looking for drugs.

SHAMANS: THE EARLY INUIT HEALERS

The main health problems affecting the early Inuit were hunger and starvation and injury. Sometimes men came home without a seal or caribou, forcing their families to go without food for days or weeks. Accidents often occurred during the hunt. Cuts would be treated by the application of spider webs and puffballs, which coagulated the blood and stopped the bleeding. Larger open wounds were treated by wrapping them with fresh animal skin. This technique helped remove gangrenous tissue. Broken bones could be treated by green bark, which formed a hard cast as it dried. Where wood was not available, animal bone was used. More serious wounds were treated by amputation using instruments at least partially sterilized by heating them with burning animal oil. The person empowered to deal with these situations was a shaman. He or she treated both physical and mental illness and was thought to have spiritual powers.

Shamans were destined to become tribal leaders from a very early age based on the perception of certain personal characteristics of the child. These included an ability to understand how the world works and how to bring order to things: "A shaman is someone able to cross the boundary separating the physical from the spiritual."[14] A future shaman could even be identified before birth: a woman who felt early labour pains before a coming disaster might conclude that the fetus was destined to become a shaman.

In times of illness, a shaman could go into a trance, enter the victim's body, and rout out the cause of the disease. Natural disasters such as storms or periods of starvation were thought to be due to the breaking of certain taboos, which could be either prevented or fixed by the shaman. The Inuit believed that illness, accidents, storms, and even poor hunting were not random events. Spirits brought them on, especially when taboos had been broken. Taboos prohibited the eating of the meat of a sea and land animal at the same meal, or the eating of fresh fish by a woman who had just delivered a baby or by a young girl who was menstruating. The spirits had to be appeased for the destructive cycle to be broken. This was the shaman's job. He did this by temporarily entering into the spirit world. "The shamans were seen the same way we [now] see doctors."[15]

THE ORIGIN OF EPIDEMICS

Most human infectious diseases probably originated in animals. Various bacterial or viral agents were transmitted to humans when animals were domesticated, beginning twelve thousand years ago or more. Within the human body the infectious agents changed (mutated) and gradually adapted themselves to causing disease. The spread of disease required close contact with a significant number of animals. The spread between humans required large numbers as in cities with crowded living conditions for upper respiratory spread, poor sanitation for fecal spread, and sexually active adults for venereal spread.[16] Viruses do not generally survive outside the human body. The death of an infected person resulted in the loss of that particular organism. Most infections were acute. If an infected person lived, a degree of immunity to that particular agent often prevented future infection.

None of the conditions for acute viral or bacterial infectious disease existed in the nomadic Inuit communities before the arrival of the white man. Neither did any natural immunity to the viruses. The scene was set for the arrival of new infections to a population without previous exposure to them and therefore no acquired immunity. The changing living conditions from small travelling bands to larger settlements and increased contact with outside travellers from areas where the diseases were well established were ideal for the outbreak of epidemics.

Smallpox appeared in Greenland in the early 1700s, carrying a mortality rate of up to 80 per cent among the Inuit. In time it brought the same devastation to the coastal Canadian Arctic. An epidemic of influenza spread through Labrador in 1842, and whooping cough was not far behind. In 1941–42 a typhoid epidemic killed 12 per cent of the Inuit population in the Pangnirtung area. Measles, generally thought to be a minor childhood disease, almost wiped out the Inuit of the Mackenzie delta of the western Arctic in the early 1900s and broke out in Pangnirtung again in 1956.

Measles and influenza also left the population more vulnerable to tuberculosis, a more chronic infectious disease. By 1950, 20 per cent of all Inuit were infected. In the 1960s most Inuit children tested as tuberculin positive, indicating that they had been exposed to the disease. A by-product of these epidemics was a loss of confidence in Inuit shamans when it became apparent that their ministrations were less effective than when dealing with cuts, broken bones, and broken taboos. This realization enhanced the authority of the whites in delivering their form of medical care.

MEDICAL CARE FROM THE SOUTH

During the early 1900s health care was provided by medical amateurs such as the missionaries, police, and even fur traders in the Hudson Bay Company posts. The first Anglican hospital was at Blacklead Island in Cumberland Sound, but it closed when the whaling station was abandoned. Dr David Livingston was one of the first full-time government employed doctors in the Arctic, making visits by dog team from his base at the Anglican nursing station in Pangnirtung just below the Arctic Circle. This station became the second Baffin hospital when the "flying bishop," Andrew Lang Fleming, raised the necessary money in England. A few nurses and one full-time doctor usually staffed the hospitals of Baffin and northern Quebec. Dr Otto Schaeffer was the last full-time pioneering doctor to make widespread visits by dog team during his stay of two years (1955–57) in Pangnirtung. Although I never met these pioneers, I encountered many of their successors.

One of my most memorable experiences in northern Quebec was meeting Daisy Watt as a patient. She was a striking white-haired Inuit woman from Kuujjuak (Fort Chimo), a self-taught nurse and interpreter who was instrumental in bringing early medical care across Nunavik. I was also privileged to meet Pauline Paton in Iqaluit. She had been a surgical nurse at the Montreal General Hospital during my internship in 1958. I recall, while assisting a senior surgeon at an operation, his saying, "Do you see that nurse? She's an Eskimo." Although she never worked in the North, Pauline must have been one of the first Inuit nurses. When I met her forty years later in the Arctic – she had moved back to her home in Iqaluit years before – she was very active in community affairs and a strong proponent of training young Inuit women to become nurses at Nunavut Arctic College. A number have now graduated and are working in the North. They are much better accepted than non-Inuktitut speaking nurses from the South. In 2005 the Inuit training program was in jeopardy because of a lack of funding, and its loss would have been a large step backward in Inuit health care. Fortunately a degree program now continues in partnership with Dalhousie University.

The next forms of health care brought from the South – ship visits, nursing stations, and then hospitals – were initially developed to combat epidemics, particularly tuberculosis. After the Second World War the Canadian government, concerned about issues of sovereignty over the Northwest Passage, northern defence during the Cold War, and the development of mineral rights across the North, began to realize that a number of Canadian citizens up there had been exploited and were dying from diseases brought from the South. Compared to the u.s. government in Alaska and the Danish government in Greenland, the Canadian government had devoted very little time or money to the welfare of its aboriginal peoples. The Americans were committed to assimilating the Alaskan Inuit. The Danish government took the opposite tack; feeling that the Eskimos living in Greenland could never be assimilated, it encouraged them instead to retain their traditional way of life. The Canadian federal government seemed at a loss to decide which path to follow and ignored its Arctic citizens for too long.

The Hudson Bay Company ship *Nascopie* began bringing medical teams to the coasts of Hudson Bay and Baffin Island, forming the Eastern Arctic Patrol in the 1930s. When the *Nascopie* sank in 1947, the larger and better medically equipped *C.D. Howe* replaced it from 1950 to 1968. The ship's annual visits to coastal Inuit settlements resulted in vaccinations, tuberculosis screening by x-ray, and the evacuation of many to southern sanatoria in Edmonton, Winnipeg, Hamilton, Montreal, and Quebec City. An Inuit song had the line, "the *C.D. Howe* has arrived, time to undress again."[17] Although many Inuit of all ages spent long periods of time – or died – in the South, the program and the invention of anti-tuberculosis drugs together were successful in bringing the tuberculosis epidemic under control. Of greater concern now is the spread of sexually transmitted diseases.

A federal government hospital with thirty beds was built in Frobisher Bay in 1958, and during the 1960s the Quebec government built hospitals in Kuujjuak and Povungnituq (Puvirnituq). The original Anglican hospital in Pangnirtung closed in 1972. All the major settlements in the Baffin region and northern Quebec now have nursing stations staffed year round by nurses and regularly visited by doctors from the hospitals. The McGill-

Baffin Project, which began in 1973, provided specialist visits to the eastern Arctic. The northern Quebec hospitals at Puvirnituq and Kuujjuak made individual arrangements for specialist visits, mostly with McGill faculty. The federal and provincial governments finally began trying to make amends for the diseases, both infectious and those produced by lifestyle changes, that whites brought to the Arctic.

9

Congenital Heart Disease

On one of my flights back to Montreal I sat beside an Inuit interpreter who was escorting a patient south. She told me that shamans once encouraged mothers to exchange young babies when crossing paths with other small nomadic tribes. The shamans recognized problems associated with inbreeding caused by marriages or liaisons between cousins. Up until a generation or two ago, Inuit marriages were arranged within families so that young people would remain close to their parents and relatives. Like many traditions of early civilizations, often enforced by religion, this increased the risk of emerging recessive traits through inbreeding. While seemingly cold hearted, advice of the shamans to exchange babies decreased the chances of recessive modes of inheritance being perpetuated by mating between close relatives.

Pediatric cardiologists made regular visits to Baffin and northern Quebec, but they rarely visited the smaller settlements because of too few patients. I frequently saw newborns in between their visits. My regular practice in Montreal was limited to adults,

Looking north from Broughton Island nursing station

so looking after babies and youngsters was one of the highlights of my work in the Arctic.

During my first visit to Broughton Island, on the west coast of Baffin Island just above the Arctic Circle (still the major northern centre for sealskin clothing) I was brought a one-month-old infant with blue lips and nail beds – a blue baby. She was not feeding well and was failing to gain weight. In medical terms she was "failing to thrive." It was clear that the major vessels coming from the heart were misconnected, with unoxygenated (venous) blood circulating through the arterial system and oxygenated (arterial) blood going to the lungs. I arranged for the baby to be transferred immediately to the Montreal Children's Hospital, where the problem was quickly corrected surgically. The youngster now leads a normal life.

GENES AND INHERITED HEART DISEASE

Congenital means "present at birth," even though the abnormality may not be recognized until later in life. The defect may be due to genetic inheritance. Modern understanding of genetics dates back to the Augustinian monk Gregor Mendel who in the mid-nineteenth century described dominant and recessive mechanisms based on the study of pea plants in his garden. Genetic abnormalities can be very complicated, as research into the mapping of the human genome has shown, but Mendel's two mechanisms are quite simple. Dominant inheritance only requires one gene from either parent for the trait to be manifest. The chance of inheriting the abnormality is then 50-50. One of the classics of dominant inheritance is the biochemical abnormality porphyria, which caused King George III of England to become progressively blind and insane, his condition a major cause of the Britain's loss of its American colonies.

A recessive genetic trait requires one gene from each parent to be manifest. The chances of recessive inheritance increase with inbreeding, as there is more likelihood of obtaining the bad gene from each parent. When the trait is on one of the mother's sex chromosomes (the x), the mother is a carrier of the trait, while it will become manifest in her male children who receive one of her x chromosomes and a y from the father. This classic sex-linked recessive mode of inheritance is shown in hemophilia, a disabling bleeding disorder that Queen Victoria passed on to a number of descendents, particularly Alexis Romanov, heir to the Russian throne.

These examples of the transmission of hemophilia and metabolic diseases occurred in royal families who were inclined to marriages arranged between cousins. The incidence of inherited heart disease remains constant in most populations at six to eight per thousand live births, but in most cases the exact method of genetic inheritance is unknown. However, when both parents are closely related, the chances of a child's inheriting the trait are much higher.

NON-GENETIC CONGENITAL HEART DISEASE

Congenital defects may be caused by the mother's exposure to a toxin, drug, or viral illness during early pregnancy. When pregnant women contract German measles during the first three months of pregnancy, the result may be a baby with eye and heart defects. When pregnant women took the drug thalidomide to counteract morning sickness, they gave birth to babies without limbs. Such causes of birth defects are now avoided since their recognition, but other factors such as alcohol or recreational drugs used by the mother are coming along to take their place, especially in modern day Aboriginal peoples.

THE HEART AS A PUMP

Unlike more complicated human organs such as the brain, liver, and kidneys, the heart has one simple function: to pump blood and thereby supply nutrients to all the tissues of the body. Venous (blue) blood, low in oxygen and nutrients and high in carbon dioxide, is brought to the right side of the heart (right atrium and right ventricle) to be pumped through a low-pressure pulmonary artery into the lungs where it gives off carbon dioxide and takes on oxygen. The oxygen-enriched blood is then returned to the left heart (left atrium and left ventricle), which pumps it under high pressure to the aorta, thus reaching all functioning organs. The coronary arteries supply oxygen and essential nutrients to the working heart muscle.

Before birth the functions of the fetal lungs and liver are performed by the mother's placenta, and connections between the pulmonary artery and aorta and between the vein from the gut and major vein leading to the right heart shunt blood away from these organs.

MANIFESTATIONS OF CONGENITAL HEART DISEASE

For the heart to function properly after birth, the pre-birth shunts must shut down, or the circulation will become overloaded on one side. Valves between the four cardiac chambers must function normally so that there will be no backflow when the ventricles contract to propel blood forward. The walls (septae) between the cardiac chambers must be intact to prevent abnormal communications and shunting of blood in one direction or the other.

Congenital heart diseases are divided into *cyanotic* (the baby is blue because unoxygenated blood is shunted from the venous to the arterial side of the circulation) and *non-cyanotic* (the baby is pink as no venous blood reaches the arterial side). Blue babies have abnormal communications either inside or outside the heart. They will not thrive and need an early diagnosis and surgical correction. Pink babies with heart abnormalities are usually recognized because of murmurs – noise caused by turbulent blood flow through an abnormal passage or valve narrowing. As long as the pink babies are growing and nursing well, they can usually be followed safely for long periods of time. The difficulty is in determining when they will require surgical treatment.

Since my time as a cardiologist in the eastern Arctic, my successors have carried cardiac ultrasound instruments with them to the North. These have greatly facilitated the diagnosis of congenital and acquired heart disease. When I was seeing patients in the Arctic, ultrasound instruments were not available to me. Fortunately in my early years (1960–62) training to be a cardiologist in England bedside diagnosis rather than technology was emphasized. I had also done some pediatric work during my research training at the University of California, San Francisco. I was therefore able to make a confident diagnosis in most cases with my eyes, hands, and stethoscope plus a chest x-ray and electrocardiogram. The blue babies were easy: they needed urgent evacuation to the South. The normally developing pink babies could be more challenging. Up to 70 per cent of children and adolescents have transient (innocent) heart murmurs that disappear by adult life. As their evacuation south with a parent or escort for more definitive diagnosis cost thousands of dollars, it was important not to recommend this treatment unnecessarily.

I have spent most of my clinical and academic life in university hospitals surrounded by cardiology fellows and colleagues with every recent technical diagnostic and therapeutic device available. My work in the Arctic was different. It was the bedside decision-making "in the trenches" that made my Arctic practice the most memorable part of my career.

COMPLETE HEART BLOCK IN AN INUIT FAMILY

A process known as electro-mechanical coupling controls the heart. An electrical signal is generated in a structure known as the sino-atrial node, located at the junction of the superior vena cava and upper part of the right atrium. This electrical current is conducted by specialized fibres through the atria to the atrioventricular node at the upper part of the septum separating the right and left ventricles. It is then conducted by further specialized fibres through the ventricles – the main pumping chambers of the heart – and causes the heart muscle to contract. If this specialized wiring is interrupted anywhere along its course, a lower signal will be generated at a slower rate or the heart will stop completely. When the heart rate becomes too slow because of this abnormality in electrical conduction, the patient complains of fatigue or may pass out or show symptoms of cardiac insufficiency (heart failure).

As an academic physician, I had always wanted to bring some heart research to the North. However, life during my consulting visits was usually too busy. I would begin working at 8:00 A.M. and not stop until the early evening, having seen thirty or more patients, many of them for the first time.

One day it occurred to me that an unusual number of patients from Cape Dorset, then a settlement of one thousand people on the southwest coast of Baffin Island, were requiring permanent cardiac pacemakers because of a purely electrical problem; they had no structural heart abnormality. The pacemaker relieved their symptoms. It then dawned on me that a number of them had the same last name. The early Dorset people had been relatively isolated from other Arctic Inuit. Could I have been witnessing a form of inherited heart block?

Heart block, an interruption of the electrical signal causing the heart to contract, is well known in association with other types of heart disease, particularly in patients with coronary heart disease and heart attacks (myocardial infarctions) where the electrical fibres are damaged from lack of blood supply. It also occurs in valvular disease and primary diseases of the cardiac muscle. Most reported cases of familial heart block were in young children. My Dorset patients did not present until their fifties, sixties, or seventies. Another example of this type of inheritance, a series of five adult patients, had been reported from South Africa in 1979 where the early Protestant church kept detailed and accurate birth records.

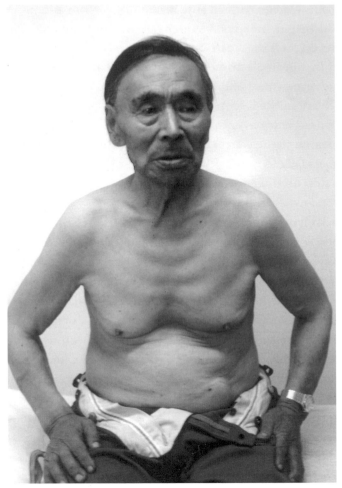

My first pacemaker patient

The problem was how to pursue this research. I was under contract to the Baffin Regional Health Board to provide cardiac consulting services, not to conduct research and spend increased time in the picturesque community of Cape Dorset, internationally known as the home of the most eminent soapstone carvers.

In 1987 I was able to obtain additional resources from the McGill Baffin project budget and arrange for one of my McGill cardiology fellows, Dr Joel Wolkowicz, to visit the community, trace family members of my pacemaker patients, and record their electrocardiograms. One advantage of the Inuit way of life is that relatives usually stayed close to their community for generations.

Unfortunately Dr Wolkowicz found that ascertaining family ties in the Inuit was more problematic than reviewing church records. The Inuit go by their first name – my patients always called me John, never Dr Burgess as in the South. Inuit originally did not have family surnames. The elders of the community gave names to Inuit babies before or after birth that would link the newborn to a favoured relative or in hope of an advantageous future trait. Nicknames referring to a personal characteristic were also common and became used instead of given names. Also, it was considered rude to refer to respected elders by name during conversation, and this too made relationships hard to confirm.[18]

Then there was the problem of poorly recorded adoptions. Unmarried teenaged girls often gave their babies to an older sister, mother, or aunt – even a grandmother. Spouses without children would be given one or more by neighbours or relatives, presumably to complete a family and to ensure they would be looked after in their old age. More than once I had women in their seventies bringing their newborns to me for examination.

All these traditions made it difficult to construct a family tree of affected patients. However, we persisted and were able to identify nine members of a family over three generations who required pacemakers during later adult life. Three more members had lesser degrees of heart block confirmed by an electrocardiogram but not yet requiring an artificial pacing device. The mode of inheritance appeared to be a dominant transmission. This represented the largest number of people with heart block and pacemakers reported in the English medical literature.[19]

A year after publication of our paper I received a telephone call from Dr Christine Seidman of Harvard University. She was internationally known in the field of cardiac molecular genetics and wanted to study my Dorset family. We arranged a three-day trip to Cape Dorset for her to obtain blood samples from over fifty presumed relatives of my patients. I remember this adventure well because it is common in the North to share double rooms in hotels with strangers because of a lack of capacity. Dr Seidman was not aware of this possibility, and I spent some time convincing the local manager that it would not be acceptable for her to bunk with a man.

I was worried about drawing blood from my patient's healthy relatives. Although I was quite adept at inserting tubes into the human heart, I had not performed the simple act of drawing blood for many years. Dr Seidman told me not to worry – she could get "blood from a stone." She proved to be right. Not one of our subjects complained of her needle sticks – most offered to give more blood if required. Unfortunately the responsible gene could not be found in our samples, and so this research remains open ended. I subsequently found a family of three in Pangnirtung all with pacemakers, but did not publish this research. Perhaps my successors will add to this number over the years, and more work can be done.

The Inuit patient I came to know best was Jonah Kelly. He had required a pacemaker because of heart block and later a mitral valve replacement. Jonah was fluently bilingual and for many years served as the radio announcer for CBC North in Iqaluit. He later became the communications officer for the Nunavut Department of Executive and Intergovernmental Affairs, a real Inuit success story. During my last visit to Iqaluit I told Jonah that I was planning to write a book about my Arctic experiences. Like my wife he was very encouraging – hence this memoir.

A LIFE-THREATENING ELECTRICAL MALFUNCTION

My most memorable Arctic cardiological problem, one I have described to first and second year medical students for over twenty years, played out at a distance. Late on a Friday afternoon I received a call from the Cape Dorset nursing station reporting that a twenty-six year old, previously healthy man with no prior history of heart disease had just come in with a heart rate of 260 per minute (the normal range is 60 to 100). He was weak and sweaty, and his blood pressure was reduced to 80/40 mm Hg. His cardiac exam was otherwise normal. I asked the nurse to immediately fax me an electrocardiogram (ECG).

When the ECG arrived about ten minutes later, it caused my own pulse rate to rise significantly. It showed what is known as an irregular wide complex tachycardia. This occurs only when there is a congenital abnormal electrical connection between the upper and lower chambers of the heart bypassing the normal conduction system. It is well known to cardiologists as the Wolfe-Parkinson-White or pre-excitation syndrome, a pure electrical abnormality occurring in structurally normal hearts. In approximately 10 per cent of these patients, the abnormal connection is capable of conducting at these extremely rapid rates, producing an acute cardiac emergency, as even the normal heart cannot sustain such a rapid rate for very long. There is insufficient time between beats for normal blood flow through the coronary arteries to the heart muscle, creating a high risk of imminent cardiac arrest and death. I called the nurse and asked her to immediately treat the young man with a direct current shock through the closed chest to correct the emergency. This could not be done as there was no regular doctor in Cape Dorset, and the nurses could not operate the electrical equipment for such a cardiac rhythm reversion.

I then called a family doctor in Iqaluit, an hour and a half distant by Twin Otter from the patient, and asked him to jump

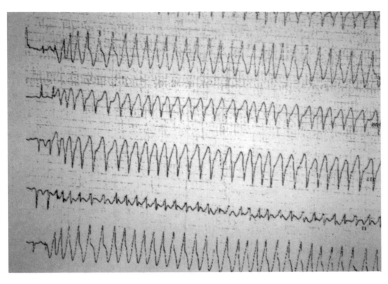

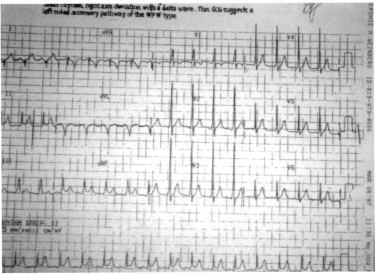

Top: Electrocardiogram of patient with life-threatening arrhythmia in Cape Dorset; heart rate is over 250 beats per minute.

Bottom: Electrocardiogram after conversion to normal rhythm and before pathway ablation

on a plane with a syringe full of procainamide. This drug would slow electrical conduction in the bypass pathway and convert the abnormal rhythm. Two hours later I received a phone call and fax ECG confirming that within ten minutes of the intravenous drug injection, the patient's heart rate had returned to normal. The ECG confirmed the diagnosis of pre-excitation. The drug was continued orally and the patient was transferred to the Montreal General Hospital. Dr Tom Hadjis, one of my younger colleagues specially trained in electrophysiology, was able to map out the offending pathway with a wire inserted into the heart and then electrically burn (ablate) it. Years later, my patient remains perfectly well with a normal heart, no medications, and a normal life expectancy. A cardiologist's life has many harrowing moments but also its rewards.

10

Valvular Heart Disease

RHEUMATIC HEART DISEASE

I met Cindy, a very attractive young Inuit, during one of my first visits to the Baffin Regional Hospital in Iqaluit. She was nineteen years old, three months pregnant with her first child, and becoming short of breath during only mild exertion. One of the family doctors referred her to me because he had heard a heart murmur and was concerned about her ability to carry on with her pregnancy.

As soon as I examined her heart, it was clear that Cindy had severe mitral stenosis, a narrowing of the valve between the left atrium and left ventricle. The left atrial chamber of the heart receives oxygenated blood from the lungs and passes it through to the left ventricle, the powerful chamber that distributes the blood to all the organs of the body. When the valve between these two chambers becomes narrowed, the pressure rises in the left atrium. This rise in pressure is transmitted backwards to the vessels draining the lungs (the pulmonary veins). The small lung vessels become congested, making the lungs stiff and harder to expand. The patient becomes short of breath.

Pregnancy causes an increase in circulating blood volume and a need for the heart to pump more blood to maintain both the mother and the growing fetus. These adaptations continue as the pregnancy progresses, and so it was clear that Cindy could not carry her baby to term. I arranged for her transfer to the Montreal General Hospital to have her pregnancy terminated. My surgical colleagues then fixed her narrowed valve. She has subsequently remained well and has delivered two healthy children.

In patients with mitral stenosis the valve narrowing may progress so slowly that symptoms remain unnoticed. When I met Andrew, a strongly built young man who looked more like a prize-fighter than a manual labourer, he was twenty-nine years old. Like Cindy, he had severe mitral stenosis, but had remained working in an open-pit lead-zinc mine in Nanisivik, a town in the far northeastern corner of Baffin Island. On careful questioning he admitted that he seemed more short of breath than his fellow workers, especially when the temperature reached -50 degrees Celsius. He continued working despite an increasing disability, as he was a proud, productive wage-earner. When I saw him after arranging for his mitral valve to be fixed, he told me that he had never realized what is was like to be able to breathe and exercise normally. Acquired narrowing of the left-sided heart valves progresses so slowly that patients often may not realize that their exercise tolerance is less than that of their friends.

During the first half of the twentieth century the commonest cause of valvular heart disease was a complication of rheumatic fever. This is still the case in many parts of the developing world, but rheumatic fever is now rare in Europe and North America. Acute rheumatic fever is caused by an immunological response to a specific type of streptococcal throat infection. It typically

Andrew Taqtu and family. Andrew worked in open pit mine in temperatures of minus 40 degrees Celcius despite severe valvular heart disease.

occurs in children between the ages of five and fifteen years, appearing several weeks after a severe sore throat. It is manifested by fever, arthritis, neurological changes, and inflammation of the heart muscle, its lining, and valves. Only the heart changes become permanent: it has been said that rheumatic fever licks the joints, but wounds the heart. The symptoms of rheumatic heart disease, particularly mitral stenosis, usually do not appear before adult life or are precipitated by the circulatory changes of pregnancy, as in Cindy's case. But recurrent bouts of rheumatic fever can result in a rapid increase in valvular damage and problems at a much earlier age, such as I frequently encountered during my early visits to the North.

Pia, a pretty but shy woman, was nearly forty years old when I saw her during my first northern visit in 1973. She had severe leaks of both her mitral and aortic valves due to several episodes of acute rheumatic fever as a child. These episodes were unrecognized, and she did not have access to medical care to prevent their

Pia Iou, the first Inuit with double heart valve replacement

recurrence. She was severely disabled by shortness of breath, and her heart was enlarging due to the overload caused by the leaking valves. She required a double valve replacement – a big decision carrying an operative mortality of greater than 10 per cent. Neither Pia nor her family had met me before, and they were initially reluctant to follow this advice despite what I thought was a detailed explanation, albeit through an interpreter.

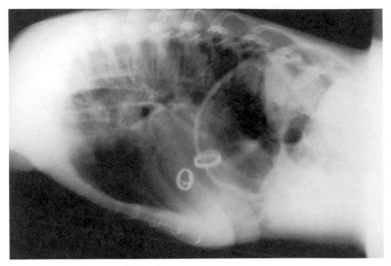

Pia Iou's X-ray of two artificial valves

Fortunately one of Pia's daughters spoke English, and she soon realized that there was really no alternative. Pia and her family returned to me the next day and agreed to come to the Montreal General Hospital for the procedure. I believe she was the first Inuit patient to have a double valve replacement. It was a great success. She lived another fifteen years relatively asymptomatic. On one of her last visits her daughter brought me an exquisite carving of a bird and egg in a nest – Pia was too shy to deliver it to me herself – saying, "She says thank you for helping her." It was the first and one of the few gifts that I ever received from a northern patient. I treasure it, because it represents an acceptance and gratitude for my work that was not always obvious in the North.

Crowded living conditions (one cough from a child with a sore throat can spread the streptococcal bugs to brothers and sisters close by), lack of early medical care, and absence of prompt treatment of a strep throat with penicillin can all predispose

people to recurrent rheumatic fever. During my cardiology training in Birmingham, I had helped run a weekly "mitral clinic." I
had a crash course there in valvular heart disease and learned its
early recognition. I saw many cases of valvular heart disease similar to Cindy's because of the crowded living conditions of the industrial British Midlands. I also saw severe valvular disease when
I was a visiting professor in Addis Ababa, Ethiopia, and while examining cardiologists in training at Baragwanath Hospital in Jo-
hannesburg, South Africa. Baragwanath Hospital is located on the
outskirts of the Soweto slum. Children brought up among many
siblings in huts and one-room dwellings were at high risk for recurrent rheumatic fever and rapidly advancing valvular heart disease. Similar social conditions existed among the Baffin Inuit
until two decades ago.

With better living conditions the incidence of rheumatic
fever, like that of tuberculosis, was already decreasing in the developed world even before the widespread introduction of antibiotics. Rheumatic valvular heart disease can be wiped out by
penicillin in two ways. I recommended that both be applied rig-
orously in Nunavut and Nunavik.

Penicillin can be given as a preventative measure at the first
signs of an acute throat infection. This was done in Costa Rica in
the early 1970s. Because of cost, throat cultures were not taken to
confirm the presence of the streptococcus; any child with symptoms and signs suggesting a streptococcal throat infection was
given a single injection of long-acting penicillin (benzathine
penicillin). Within a decade of the initiation of these measures,
rheumatic fever and its subsequent valvular disease were virtually eliminated in Costa Rica.[20]

The second method is to use penicillin prophylactically until
early adult life to prevent the recurrent episodes that destroyed
Pia's two heart valves. Daily oral doses of penicillin effectively prevent recurrent rheumatic fever and progressive valve damage.

The problem is to ensure patient compliance, especially in adolescents and young adults who do not have close parental supervision. A monthly intramuscular injection has the advantage of ensuring the penicillin is on board, but with the drawback that it leaves the patient with a sore backside for one to two days – perhaps a greater stimulus to non-compliance. My challenge was to convince the youngster or young adult that whatever the degree of the present valve problem, it would not get worse if the penicillin was taken, and a future valve repair could be either delayed or avoided.

During the next two decades of my career in Arctic cardiology I saw no new cases of acute rheumatic fever and no rheumatic valvular disease such as Cindy's. As with most diseases, it is much better to prevent the problem rather than to deal with it imperfectly after it arises.

NON-RHEUMATIC VALVULAR HEART DISEASE

The fairly rapid decline in the incidence of rheumatic fever left me to deal with non-rheumatic causes of valvular disease – some increasing in frequency as the population ages.

Mitral Valve Insufficiency

Congenital abnormalities of the valve leaflets and their attachments are now the commonest cause of mitral insufficiency. In contrast to the narrowed valve of mitral stenosis, these abnormalities can produce a progressive leak, thereby overloading the left ventricle in its attempt to maintain forward flow. The patient usually remains asymptomatic for many years before the heart starts to fail, but must be closely followed to ensure that the valve is repaired or replaced before irreversible damage is done to the overloaded muscle. I would arrange to see the patient semi-annually

Ida Karpik, one of Nunavut's most famous artists, followed for
twenty-five years with leaking heart valve

during my regular trips North and consider further investigation
and surgery if the left ventricle began to dilate. I determined this
by bedside examination and chest x-ray, but ultrasound technology has now made the task easier.

Tricuspid Insufficiency

The tricuspid valve separates the right atrium (the chamber receiving blood from the great veins returning to the heart) from
the right ventricle (which pumps the venous blood to the lungs
where oxygen is added and carbon dioxide given off). One of my
favourite patients was Ida Karpik. She was born with a leaking tricuspid valve, but as it was on the low-pressure right hand side of
her heart, it did not cause her any disability other than a flushed
red face and mild swelling of her legs.

Ida lived in Pangnirtung, the gateway to entry into the Arctic
Circle and the home of artists (particularly watercolourists) and
weavers. Ida was an accomplished painter. I followed her regularly during my semi-annual visits to "Pang" for twenty-five years.
She died following heart surgery at the age of sixty-three after my
Baffin visits had come to an end. Her passing was reported in the
Nunatsiaq News, where she was recognized as "one of the original
artists ... Karpik left her mark on both the hamlet and arts community."[21] She had been born in a small High Arctic settlement
but, like many Inuit, had moved from a camp on Cumberland
Sound to the larger town of Pangnirtung in 1964 to be near her
children who were attending school. She began to draw seriously
in 1974 and for twenty-eight years produced hundreds of drawings on paper, showing different aspects of traditional Inuit life,
birds, and animals. Many of her drawings are in the archives at
the Uqqurmiut Centre for Arts and Crafts in Pangnirtung.[22] I
have a beautiful coloured print of Inuit people, birds, and seals
on an ice-floe done by Ida's sister Leah, but unfortunately none
of Ida's work. She will remain a legendary artist of the North. I
am proud to have been her cardiologist for all of my years serving Baffin.

Johanassie, aortic stenosis patient

Aortic Stenosis

I first encountered Johanassie, a fifty-five year old porter at the
Baffin Regional Hospital, because he was getting dizzy and light-
headed during exertion. On one occasion he passed out while
climbing the stairs to the in-patient ward. He was referred to me
because of a heart murmur, which had been present since childhood but had never previously caused any trouble.

On cardiac examination Johanassie had a heaving apex beat through the chest wall indicating an increased left ventricular muscle mass, a slow upstroke in the carotid artery indicating obstruction to outflow through the aortic valve, and a loud ejection murmur characteristic of severe aortic stenosis (a narrowed aortic valve impeding blood flow from the left ventricle to the aorta). He had been born with two instead of three leaflets in his aortic valve. This abnormality caused turbulent flow through the valve, and over the years had resulted in thickening, calcification, and progressive narrowing.

Aortic stenosis is virtually never rheumatic in origin. Patients like Johanassie are characteristically asymptomatic for many years. When symptoms such as dizziness, fainting, chest pain, or shortness of breath develop, there is a high risk of rapid deterioration and sudden death. I arranged for Johanassie to be admitted to the Montreal General Hospital, where he had his valve replaced with a mechanical one. Subsequent to his valve replacement he developed tuberculosis, a reactivation of an earlier infection, but fortunately this was cleared with appropriate long-term antibiotic treatment, and he has remained well since.

Congenital valvular disease can be associated with other abnormalities. I first saw Emily when she was four years old. She had Williams Syndrome, a group of features consisting of mental retardation, a characteristic elfin face, and continual fidgeting and laughing. The latter symptoms give rise to the name "cocktail party syndrome." These patients also have a narrowing above the aortic valve. It is a difficult decision to recommend cardiac surgery and valve replacement in a child with a reduced life expectancy. I have usually advised it when the youngster appears to have a good quality of life. Fortunately, Emily did not have any symptoms from her supravalvular aortic stenosis, and I was able to follow her for a number of years. The chances are that her valve will not need replacing during her lifetime.

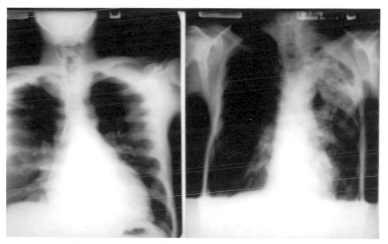

Johanassie: (left) X-ray before aortic valve replacement; (right) after valve replacement, heart size now normal but tuberculosis in left upper lung field

Emily, a young girl with Williams Syndrome – elfin face, perpetual smile, and aortic stenosis.

My oldest patient; a granddaughter said she was in her nineties.

Congenital aortic stenosis can be very severe, resulting in symptoms early in life. Diane was only twelve when I saw her because of the onset of heart failure. She required urgent aortic valve replacement as no combination of pills can overcome this mechanical problem preventing the outflow of blood from the left ventricle. Patients with mechanical heart valves require long-term anticoagulants (blood thinners); otherwise, clots will form on the metal surface. Diane went to the Montreal Children's

Hospital, where doctors made the decision to replace her aortic valve with a tissue one (a pig/Hancock valve), which obviates the need for lifelong anticoagulants. This was an unfortunate choice, as we subsequently learned that tissue valves have a short lifespan, especially in young people, although they remain the replacement of choice in the elderly whose life expectancy is less than that of the implanted valve – usually ten to fifteen years. Diane's tissue valve failed within five years, and she had to have a mechanical replacement requiring a second heart operation.

Artificial valves are never as good as the originals. They are prone to failure and infection. This is the reason we cannot go prophylactically replacing valves in asymptomatic patients. Diane's mechanical valve was leaking when I last saw her. I could hardly bear to tell her that she would need it replaced sometime in the future. She moved away from Nunavut, and I lost contact with her, but I am sure she feels that she has not benefited from my or my colleagues' care. Fortunately I have had many more Inuit patients with outcomes like Cindy and Johanassie than that of Diane.

Aortic Insufficiency

One of my most memorable valve disease patients was Nala, a tall, striking-looking Inuit woman in her thirties. Her husband, Brent Body, worked at the Baffin Regional Hospital and as a sideline kept husky dogs on an island in Frobisher Bay. He became well known as an outfitter and guide for Arctic tourists, but his main claim to fame was that he was a member of the Steger expedition that travelled to the North Pole. In March 1986 Will Steger led seven men and one woman to the pole by dog sled without any resupply along the way.[23] Brent was awarded the Order of Canada in 1987. The presentation was at Government House in May 1988.

Nala's aortic valve leak had become very severe, and she required an urgent aortic valve replacement a few weeks before the event. However, she insisted on being present only weeks after her open-heart surgery to see Brent being presented to Governor-General Jeanne Sauvé. After the ceremony and before dinner Nala felt faint near the entranceway of Rideau Hall. Coincidentally I was present to receive the Order of Canada for my work in the Arctic and my research and teaching at McGill University. I was summoned by her husband and father-in-law and raised a number of eyebrows by examining her in the vestibule. Fortunately no serious heart event had occurred, and the gala evening continued. I am probably the only cardiologist to have looked after a patient in the presence of the governor-general and many newly invested members of the Order of Canada.

11

Infective Endocarditis

Any damage to the linings of heart valves or defects in the septae separating the heart chambers increases the risk of infection occurring on these surfaces. Normal heart tissues are rarely affected except in the case of intravenous drug users. A transient release of bacteria into the bloodstream, often from an infection in the mouth (gums) or less frequently from the gut or urinary tract, initiates the infection. Various bacteria and other infectious organisms can colonize these areas and produce rapidly progressive damage to the structure, resulting in the valve becoming insufficient or the hole between heart chambers becoming larger. In addition, the bacteria can spread throughout the body via the bloodstream, producing abscesses in such vital organs as the brain and kidneys. Such an infection on the interior lining of heart structures is known as infective endocarditis. It can produce a sudden worsening of the original abnormality and the onset of heart failure.

The reason for tooth decay and risk of infective endocarditis

Patients with artificial valves are predisposed to virulent organisms, staphylococci, pneumococci, and others, which can
cause a rapidly progressive infection known as acute bacterial endocarditis. A more common form is subacute endocarditis, usually caused by streptococcus viridans, an organism normally in
the mouth. This is a particular problem in the Inuit resulting
from poor oral and dental hygiene.

Tristan da Cuhna, a British protectorate, one of a group of
four small islands in the south Atlantic, offers an instructive parallel. It is the most remote inhabited island in the world with
about 250 residents. When I was training in England in 1961, a
volcanic eruption forced the evacuation of all its citizens to England. When they arrived, none had ever owned a toothbrush,
nor did any have dental cavities or gum disease. This did not last
long once they were introduced to British corner sweet shops – the

hard candies rapidly took their toll. Fifteen years later I learned that this situation was relevant to the Inuit. Women had traditionally worn down their teeth chewing skins to make them more tender, but they did not have cavities or gum disease. The southerners' introduction of sugary confectionaries and other foods rapidly created a widespread problem, especially in the absence of regular dental checkups or parental insistence on tooth brushing. This posed a real risk for the development of infective endocarditis in those with congenital or acquired valve disease or other heart abnormalities.

There are two ways to decrease the risk of infective endocarditis. One is dental prophylaxis – the regular cleaning of teeth and gums with a toothbrush to prevent plaque buildup and avoid the constant bath of sugar from candies and soft drinks. I became very friendly with Dr Marc Levesque, the senior dentist in Iqaluit, and used to complain to him about the state of my patients' teeth and their risk for infection.

"You get them to come to me and I can fix the problem," he said, but this was easier said than done. An encounter with a dentist's drill is not a happy occasion in any civilization. I found it difficult to convince adults that their dental care was just as important as my heart treatment, although I was usually successful in having appropriate repairs and extractions done prior to cardiac surgery.

A second method of endocarditis prophylaxis is similar to that of rheumatic fever prophylaxis. One dose of penicillin an hour before any dental procedure will usually provide satisfactory protection. This can be easier to enforce, as the dentist can insist on the antibiotic prior to treatment if he knows that the patient has a heart problem presenting a risk for endocarditis.

The subacute form of infective endocarditis can be very insidious. Before the antibiotic era of the 1950s, it was uniformly

fatal. Now most cases can be cured by several weeks of appropriate intravenous antibiotics as long as the diagnosis is made before there is extensive destruction of the heart valve

One of my patients was a respected village elder from Apex,
a small settlement several kilometres down the peninsula from
Iqaluit. He had stable and relatively mild disease of two of his
heart valves. He was sent to my outpatient clinic because of a
slight fever and general malaise. His heart murmurs had wors-
ened, suggesting a recent and ongoing infection. I explained to
him that this was curable, but he would have to be admitted to
hospital for several weeks. He was reluctant to agree to this, in
part because of his advanced age. I tried to enlist the help of his
son and daughter who accompanied him, explaining the serious-
ness of the problem if it was not correctly diagnosed and treated.
He insisted on returning home to think it over. He did not return
and later died in intractable heart failure caused by his rapidly
deteriorating valves. Nothing is more frustrating for a physician
than to have his treatment plan refused, especially for a potentially curable condition. I have often had second thoughts as to
how I could have better handled this problem. An Inuit physician or nurse might have been more successful in knowing the
right words to convince the patient or in reassuring him that my
advice would be of benefit.

12

Pulmonary Heart Disease

The only house call that I ever made during my Arctic trips was in Inukjuak, about halfway up the east coast of Hudson Bay. My patient was seventy-seven years old and well known in the community as a once-eminent hunter. As a young man he had lived in the Pond Inlet area of Nunavut near the northern tip of Baffin Island. For many years he had been exposed to very cold conditions both on seal and polar bear hunts. He had learned to smoke from the white traders, but had stopped over twenty years earlier. When I saw him he was so short of breath that he could not venture out of his house and had to breathe oxygen from a tank twenty-four hours a day. If he removed the mask from his face, his fingers and lips became blue from lack of oxygen, and I did not need my stethoscope to hear the loud wheezing as he struggled to breathe. He required almost constant care from a daughter and granddaughter.

Despite his very poor quality of life he smiled at my entrance and seemed grateful that I had come to his home to try to help him. Unfortunately his problem was so far advanced that there was little I could do except to continue his home oxygen, treat flare-ups of his lung infection with antibiotics, and give him diuretics to reduce his uncomfortable leg swelling.

His problem was pulmonary heart disease (cor pulmonale), a form of heart failure secondary to a primary disorder of the airspaces in the lung or its vessels. Worldwide this condition is nearly always caused by chronic bronchitis (a productive cough) and emphysema (dilatation of the small airways of the lung, accompanied by an irreversible destruction of their walls). These two progressive changes impair the addition of oxygen to the blood entering the lungs and the simultaneous removal of carbon dioxide. As a result the pressure in the pulmonary arteries supplying blood to the lungs increases and the right-sided chambers of the heart begin to fail, causing fluid retention in the abdomen and lower extremities.

Chronic bronchitis and emphysema, usually lumped together under the term chronic obstructive lung disease (COPD), is the most common disabling respiratory condition in the developed world and is closely linked to cigarette smoking. The problem is hardly ever seen in the South, except in patients who have smoked one to two packages of cigarettes daily for ten or more years. There is no doubt that this relatively recently acquired habit in the Inuit is a factor in causing COPD. However, I found it more frequent in more northern hunters exposed to very cold air than in the more southern town-dwellers who tended to smoke even more.

Dr Otto Schaefer, the pioneering medical researcher of the Canadian Arctic, first noticed this association during the 1970s. He and his colleagues found evidence of airway obstruction and elevation of right heart pressures in the older and more northern Inuit hunters and coined the terms "frozen lung," "Eskimo lung," and "Eskimo heart." I had been taught in medical school that inhaled air reached body temperature by the time it hit the back of the throat. Although this might be true for southern urban dwellers, it may not apply to Arctic hunters, often exercising at temperatures around 40 below Celsius. Dr Schaefer concluded that, contrary to previously held beliefs, the forced cold air inhalation was the main cause of the pulmonary heart disease in northern Inuit hunters.[24] However, there is no doubt that continued cigarette smoking causes a more rapid progression of the problem, and complete cessation heads the top of the treatment list. I was sometimes tempted to tell my northern medical colleagues not to ask their patients with chronic obstructive lung disease to stop smoking before I saw them in consultation, for otherwise I would have no other useful advice to offer.

As I noticed the increase in cigarette smoking among younger Inuit during my years of northern travel, I worried that the incidence of "Eskimo lung" might not decrease even as global warming lessens the amount of Arctic hunting. It is discouraging to think that as a traditional way of Arctic life is threatened by southern global pollution and warming, cigarettes may replace cold air inhalation as a cause of "Eskimo heart."

13

Cardiomyopathy

Daisy was two and a half years old when I first saw her. She had been down to the Montreal Children's Hospital six months before with a very large heart, congested lungs, and swelling of her abdomen and legs. The cause of her heart failure was cardiomyopathy, a primary disorder of the heart muscle reducing its ability to pump sufficient blood for the needs of her body. Unlike heart failure caused by congenital defects, valvular disease, high blood pressure, or coronary artery disease causing recurrent heart attacks, cardiomyopathy is of unknown cause. It may follow a respiratory virus infection. In such cases, about one-third will spontaneously improve and be left with a healed and normal muscle. Daisy was one of the lucky ones. With bed rest and appropriate medicines, she gradually improved and was able to return home to Iqaluit. She became a perfectly healthy normal little girl. I was gradually able to stop her medication as her heart returned to normal size and her exercise tolerance increased. When I last saw

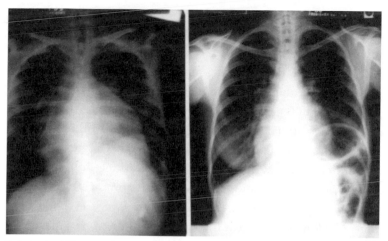

Daisy's chest X-rays before and after resolution of viral cardiomyopathy. Left: large heart at two years of age; right: normal-sized heart after spontaneous resolution three years later

her, she had no evidence of any prior heart problem. She likely now leads a normal life and has a family of her own.

Joe was not so lucky. He was abandoned by his parents in Pond Inlet during his early teens and became addicted to alcohol before many Arctic settlements became dry. Ten ounces of alcohol daily for ten years can permanently damage the heart and liver. His heart muscle became irreversibly damaged, and his lungs, like Daisy's, became congested, making him increasingly short of breath. He experienced only slight improvement after giving up alcohol and taking appropriate medications.

In the absence of a remedial cause for a patient's heart failure, cardiac transplantation was a consideration. However, this requires lifelong drugs and close follow-up to prevent rejection – not an option at that time in the High Arctic. Joe was not willing to move permanently to the South. Even if he had agreed to consider transplantation, the chances were greater than 50 per cent that he would die before a suitable donor heart could be found, and his life expectancy after successful transplantation was only about 50 per cent for five years. Joe was on a progressively downhill course. After considering all the options, he decided on a new experimental procedure using transformed skeletal muscle to assist the failing heart muscle.

When a human or animal exercises, the working skeletal muscles gradually fatigue and must be rested. The heart has special muscle fibres known as "slow twitch," which do not fatigue. Otherwise our heart could not continually contract 60-100 times per minute – more during exercise and times of stress – for a lifetime. Dr "Ray" C.J. Chiu at the Montreal General Hospital and a few other researchers conceived the idea that skeletal muscle could be trained to behave like normal heart muscle by repetitive electrical stimulation. This technique proved to be successful in experimental animals, and the technique of dynamic cardiomyoplasty was born. The patient's latissimus dorsi muscle from the left side of the back is isolated, leaving its nerves and blood supply intact. It is then moved and wrapped around the failing heart. An artificial pacemaker is attached, which senses the normal electrical activity of each heart-beat, and then delivers five short bursts to the transplanted skeletal muscle. In about two weeks this stimulated muscle wrap appears to assist the ventricle in augmenting its blood flow, significantly improving the patient's symptoms.

Dr Chiu, along with other surgical colleagues at the Montreal General and I, had carried out dynamic cardiomyoplasty on seven patients who were not suitable candidates for transplantation. It was an exciting alternative to transplantation, although we were uncertain as to how long the early benefits would last. We were part of a multi-centre trial approved by the National Institutes of Health in North America. Joe became our fifth patient and the only Aboriginal to have the procedure. He was much improved and able to return to his home in the north of Baffin Island. I would see him in Iqaluit twice yearly and he would come to Montreal every three months to have his pacemaker checked. The only evidence of his prior heart disease was the large scars on his back and left chest and the twitching muscle in his right armpit before it entered his chest. He told me that he quickly got used to that sensation and that it no longer bothered him.

Patients with various types of heart muscle disorders are at risk of sudden electrical abnormalities causing a cardiac arrest. We had tried with limited success to control this problem with drugs and defibrillator devices that would correct the cardiac arrest. Joe lived for four years, but then died suddenly at his home. He always greeted me with a smile and never regretted our decision, which gave him four more years of a relatively happy life. As the medical management of heart failure subsequently improved, dynamic cardiomyoplasty has been abandoned, but it was a significant, if temporary, benefit for Joe and several of my other patients.

14

Coronary Artery Disease

During my early years as consultant cardiologist, when I was called about a patient with chest pain in the Baffin Region, my first question was: "Is the person Inuit or white?" If the answer was Inuit, my first thought was that the chest discomfort was probably not due to the heart. As time went on, this assumption no longer held true.

Coronary heart disease, technically known as coronary atherosclerosis, results from accumulating plaque in the arterial vessels supplying the heart muscle. It takes many years before it becomes manifest, as the interior of the artery must be reduced to 30 per cent of normal before blood flow is compromised and chest discomfort known as angina becomes manifest. Angina often occurs when the heart is stressed by exercise or emotion, producing an increase in heart rate. It is not the severe obstructions that cause acute coronary events – heart attacks and sudden death – but the narrowings of 50 per cent or less with a soft lipid centre that suddenly rupture. When this occurs, blood platelets aggregate and a

One of my first patients with coronary artery disease

clot forms, occluding the artery and causing the loss of heart muscle. These minor narrowings are undetectable until a sudden event occurs. It is possible for accumulating atherosclerotic plaque to remain unrecognized for decades.

The famous Framingham study, begun in 1948 in Framingham, Massachusetts, demonstrated that coronary artery disease was associated with a number of things that came to be known as risk factors. The non-modifiable ones were increasing age, male gender, and family history. Potentially modifiable major risk factors were high blood cholesterol levels, high blood pressure, and cigarette smoking. Any one of these doubled the risk of coronary disease, and when all three were present, the risk to an individual was increased over six-fold. Diabetes, lack of physical exercise, and stress were later added. The shocking discovery of significant coronary plaque in young American soldiers killed during the Korean War in the early 1950s brought lifestyle, especially diet, to the forefront.

The conventional wisdom until the latter half of the twentieth century was that the Inuit people were protected from coronary disease because of their lifestyle. The lack of coronary disease in the Inuit was noted by early Arctic explorers and later by physicians studying the Greenland Inuit. In the early 1900s the most frequent cause of death in the Greenland Eskimo was tuberculosis, followed by accidents, and then pneumonia. In the widely quoted study by Bertelsen and colleagues, coronary heart disease was not even mentioned.[25] However, although most agreed that the incidence of atherosclerotic disease was less prevalent in the Inuit than in whites living in the North, its absence has been disputed. Laboratory tests for its detection such as electrocardiograms were not employed, autopsies were rarely performed, and death certificates were frequently signed without the body being seen.

When I first began my northern visits in 1973, I did not see any cases of manifest coronary disease, but I began to recognize it during the 1980s. Even in the early 1990s, "the Northwest Territories age-standardized mortality rate for ischemic (coronary) heart disease was consistently lower than the rate for Canada."[26] By mid-decade, coronary heart disease in the Inuit equalled the all-Canadian rate: "In Canada's two regions with predominantly

Inuit populations, Nunavik and Nunavut, the age-adjusted mortality rates in 1995–1997 for all cardiovascular diseases were … not significantly different from the all-Canadian rate."[27] Whether or not coronary heart disease was absent or rare in the Inuit during the first half of the twentieth century, it was certainly increasing rapidly during the second half. As Dr Otto Schaefer has said, "Few people have ever experienced such drastic changes in their way of living and dying as did the Eskimos and Indians in the Canadian north … Those eating the traditional diet of game and fish got all the protein that they needed, and most of the calories, with little (saturated) fat – they thrived. In contrast, those who ate chocolate bars, potato chips, soft drinks and high-calorie starchy foods from the stores, were paying a heavy price."[28]

Junk food, introduced relatively recently to the Arctic, is high in saturated and trans fats, which increase the bad cholesterol (LDL), decrease the good cholesterol (HDL), increase the damaging inflammatory process in the coronary arteries, and reduce their ability to dilate. Trans fats are found in deep-fried fast foods, bakery products, and packaged fast foods. Junk foods such as non-diet soft drinks are also a major cause of childhood and adolescent obesity. The Inuit were falling prey to the diseases of civilization. A recent study of the Inuit of northern Quebec (Nunavik) confirmed this trend: "Evidence points to decreasing traditional food consumption by younger Inuit. Thus, the promotion of safe nutritional habits among Inuit presents a two-fold challenge: maintain or increase traditional food use, which confers a comparative advantage to the Inuit population (e.g., low IHD – ischemic heart disease – mortality rate), and support efforts to increase the use of healthy market foods."[29]

Dr I.M. Rabinowitch of the Montreal General Hospital made the earliest Canadian observations on heart disease in the Inuit of the eastern Arctic. He was head of the Metabolism department and mainly interested in diabetes and nutrition. As both

are important risk factors for atherosclerotic disease, his observations are pertinent to today's coronary health in the Inuit. His
seminal paper in the *Canadian Medical Association Journal* in 1936
has been largely overlooked.[30] Dr Rabinowitch spent several
months on the Canadian Government Eastern Arctic Patrol aboard
the ship *Nascopie.* He visited the east and west coasts of Hudson
Bay, the south and west coasts of Baffin Island, and as far north
as Devon and Ellsmere Islands. At that time there were about
2,400 Inuit in the area; Dr Rabinowitch's studies included about
15 per cent of them. In Baffin the patrol visited five ports: Cape
Dorset, Lake Harbour, Pangnirtung, Pond Inlet, and Clyde River.
Dr Rabinowitch obtained blood sugar curves to test for diabetes
along with x-rays of the lower extremities, looking for calcification indicating atherosclerosis. He noted during his journey that
the more northern Inuit lived in the more primitive conditions,
while those in the South were more influenced by the white
man's way of life and diet. Animal products (seal and fish) were
the main food staples in the northern outposts, while flour was
common in the South. He also noted that while tooth-brushing
was more common in the South, the more northern Inuit had
healthier teeth, presumably because of less dietary sugar. His con-
clusion was that atherosclerosis frequently occurred in the southern parts of the Eastern Canadian Arctic where contact with
whites had changed the Inuit diet, but in the more northern settlements cholesterol was low and atherosclerosis absent because
the traditional diet was still consumed.[31]

Dr Rabinowitch's most important finding was evidence of
only six cases of atherosclerosis in the Baffin Inuit, whereas in
the Hudson Bay area nineteen of thirty-nine x-rays showed evidence of calcification of the lower extremity arteries – an incidence of nearly 50 per cent. He found practically no evidence of
diabetes in either area, almost certainly due to the absence of
overweight and obesity at that time. Dr Rabinowitch was very

perceptive in seeing the effects of the southerners' way of life and diet on the future health of the Inuit:

It is its [the Hudson Bay Company] policy to encourage the Eskimo to live as much as possible in his native state; he is encouraged to live in tents, to confine his diet to the animal food of his environment and to clothe himself with the furs of these animals. Unfortunately, the unrelenting laws of evolution apply to the Eskimo as elsewhere, and, it is obvious that this practice must, with time, become more and more difficult. As the motorboat is replacing the kayak, and the gun the harpoon, so must the habits of diet change. Civilized man's foods are more palatable than native foods, and the Eskimo not only knows of their existence, but he has also tasted them. In my opinion, however, this change is not incompatible with health.[32]

As atherosclerosis is a slowly developing disease, it took another forty years to show that this opinion was incorrect.

Dr H.M. Sinclair made important observations on the lack of coronary atherosclerosis in the Inuit in 1944. He noted that they consumed a very high fat diet but had low blood cholesterols because the fat in marine animals in cold climates was highly unsaturated. He also postulated that the traditional Inuit diet was low in substances that cause platelets to clump (omega-6 fatty acids), resulting in a clot forming on ulcerated plaque, producing heart attacks, but that it was high in omega-3 fatty acids, which decreased platelet stickiness.

Dr Sinclair did a unique experiment on himself. For one hundred days he ate nothing but marine animal food (seal, fish, crustaceans, and molluscs) and drank only water. His blood cholesterol and all four lipoproteins (Very Low Density Cholesterol (VLDL), Intermediate Density Cholesterol (IDL) and Low Density

Cholesterol (LDL) – the atherogenic lipids – fell dramatically. His High Density Cholesterol (HDL) – the anti-atherogenic lipid fraction – increased, and his platelet count fell. His "bleeding time rose from the normal value of three to four minutes to about fifty minutes and then declined to about fifteen minutes; epistaxis (nosebleeds) and spontaneous bleeding occurred." This latter observation was in keeping with what I had been told about more bleeding in Inuit after delivering children.[33]

Sinclair's work and that done by others subsequently proved that fatty fish high in omega acids – especially cold-water fish – lower the bad (LDL) cholesterol and increase the good (HDL) cholesterol as well as decreasing platelet aggregation, the final factor in a coronary artery occlusion. We now know that regular exercise (another change in recent Inuit lifestyle) is the most effective way of elevating HDL cholesterol. Dr Sinclair showed not only that the traditional Inuit diet protected against coronary heart disease but that it was also an excellent way to lose weight. During the one hundred days his weight fell from ninety-six kilograms to eighty-four.

RISK FACTORS

Since the 1948 Framingham study[34] and the international Seven Country Study,[35] a number of predisposing factors (now known as risk factors) for coronary heart disease have been universally recognized. They apply to all world populations and particularly to the relatively recent changes in Inuit lifestyle. These risk factors are as follows:

Major modifiable
• High blood pressure, a major risk factor for heart attack and most important for stroke

- High blood lipids – LDL cholesterol, triglycerides, and low HDL cholesterol – increase both the likelihood of a coronary event and stroke
- Cigarette smoking, especially in people who start at a young age
- Physical inactivity – increases risk of heart disease and stroke by 50 per cent
- Obesity – major risk for coronary heart disease and adult onset diabetes
- Diabetes
- Unhealthy diet – low fruit and vegetable (fibre) intake, high saturated fat intake – increases the risk of coronary events and stroke through its effects on blood lipids and thrombosis (clotting)

Minor modifiable
- Low social and economic status
- Psychological stress
- Alcohol use: one to two drinks a day may be cardioprotective, but more can damage heart muscle
- Postmenopausal hormone replacement

Non-modifiable risk factors
- Increasing age: most heart attacks occur after age sixty-five, and stroke risk doubles every decade after fifty-five
- Family history: risk increased if a first-degree relative has had a heart attack under the age of fifty-five years
- Gender: risk is lower in pre-menopausal females, the same after menopause

THE METABOLIC SYNDROME

The metabolic syndrome is comprised of five characteristics:

1 Abdominal obesity. This is not the pear-shaped excess weight – the women with voluptuous thighs preferred by Renaissance painters – but the person with a fat belly overhanging his or her (usually his) waist. More precisely, abdominal obesity is present in men with a waist circumference greater than 102 cm (40 inches) and in women with whose waist is greater than 88 cm (35 inches). During my years as Arctic cardiologist, several Inuit patients and friends told me that before the white man came north, there was no such thing as a fat Inuk.

2 Elevated triglycerides. This characteristic is highly correlated with obesity and a high carbohydrate food intake.

3 Reduced HDL-C. Reduced "good" cholesterol is highly associated with a lack of physical exercise, a steadily increasing problem in the Inuit over the last several decades.

4 Increased blood pressure. This is related to obesity, high alcohol intake, and increased dietary salt intake. When people increase their use of prepared foods (especially canned goods, fast foods, and snacks), they lose control over their salt intake as well as calories.

5 Elevated blood sugar. This is a risk factor for coronary events even before overt diabetes is present. Again it is strongly related to obesity.

When I was training in Birmingham in the early 1960s, there was a large immigration of Southeast Asians into the area. My colleagues and I noticed that a significant number were developing heart attacks in their early forties and fifties. They did not smoke and had relatively low total blood cholesterols, so the cause was not obvious. It subsequently became apparent that they had all the manifestations of the metabolic syndrome, which has become the greatest modern risk factor for atherosclerotic disease worldwide.

INCIDENCE OF CORONARY HEART DISEASE INCREASES IN MY NORTHERN PRACTICE

Ben was in his mid-fifties. He did not smoke, but he had a large abdomen, a sedentary lifestyle, high blood cholesterol, and elevated blood pressure – all elements of the metabolic syndrome. He had been perfectly well until suddenly developing a severe, long-lasting pressure in the centre of his chest characteristic of an acute heart attack (myocardial infarction). An electrocardiogram faxed to me confirmed the diagnosis.

After his initial recovery, Ben developed angina at low levels of exercise despite optimal medical management (diet and medication). I brought him to the Montreal General Hospital where coronary angiograms showed a complete occlusion of one vessel and obstructions in several others. He underwent coronary artery bypass surgery to relieve his symptoms. He subsequently was able to be more regularly active than before his heart attack.

After Ben, I saw an increasing number of Inuit patients with manifestations of coronary artery disease – angina and heart attacks – both in the Baffin region and in northern Quebec. Most of them had risk factors for the disease. My original thought that chest pain in the Inuit was not due to the heart became untenable. Fortunately, I was able to manage most cases by lifestyle changes and medications, the former being more difficult to achieve, especially when giving advice through an interpreter. It is easier to take a pill than to change long-standing habits, no matter what your race, where you live, or what language you speak.

Following the increase in frequency of heart attacks, I arranged for a thrombolytic (clot dissolving) drug to be available in all nursing stations where a doctor was regularly present in

Baffin and northern Quebec. By the early 1980s this treatment had been shown to reduce the amount of heart muscle damage and improve mortality following a heart attack. The improvement in outcome was only achieved when the agent was given intravenously within the first six hours after the onset of symptoms. There was no time to transfer the patient to Montreal.

Within the first month of these arrangements I received a phone call and a faxed electrocardiogram from Inukjuak on the east coast of Hudson Bay. A forty-five-year-old man had chest discomfort of less than two hours' duration, and his electrocardiogram confirmed the early stages of an acute heart attack. I asked the doctor to immediately begin an infusion of the thrombolytic drug. Within an hour the patient's chest discomfort had disappeared, and the cardiogram had returned to nearly normal. This was probably one of the first successful cases of thrombolytic therapy in the Arctic, and it resulted in a very successful outcome for the patient.

The future challenge in the Arctic is to reduce the risk factors that southerners have introduced to the Inuit people and to thereby decrease the frequency of a mostly preventable disease.

15

Auyuittuq Park: An Arctic Holiday

In my thirty years of visits to the North, the only time I visited the Arctic during the summer was in 1984. Andrea and I had back-packed and camped with our children in the parks of the California and Washington coasts, climbed mountains in Banff and Jasper, and camped across Canada. We had visited game parks in Australia and South Africa and climbed Table Mountain in Cape Town. Our greatest outdoor experience, however, was the five days Andrea and I spent in Auyittuq, when we saw the world's most beautiful entrance into the Arctic Circle.

The Inukitut word "Auyuittuq" means "where the land never melts." It has also been translated as "forever on the edge of winter," "the place of the big ice," and "the land entirely without summer" – apt descriptions of Canada's only arctic national park, but ones that could change with increasing global warming. Auyittuq National Park was created in 1972. It lies mostly within the Arctic Circle, 2,400 kilometres northeast of Montreal, and is

Local inhabitants meeting aircraft arrivals in Pangnirtung

the least visited of Canada's national parks, with about 250 visitors per year when we entered it.

I had arranged to take the extra time during the first week of August before one of my twice-yearly consultation visits to Iqaluit and Pangnirtung. We flew by jet to Iqaluit and then by Twin Otter to Pangnirtung, making a 180-degree turn below mountain peaks before landing on a gravel runway. The spectacular mountains of Auyittuq were created sixty million years ago by the massive uplift of the earth's crust along the east coast of North America caused by the continental drift that separated Greenland from Baffin Island. The glaciers coming down from the Barnes and Penny Icecaps to form valleys with their fast-flowing rivers then sculpted this uplift.

We were taken by freighter canoe manned by an Inuit guide and his son thirty kilometres up Pangnirtung Fiord to Camp Overlord, the entrance into the park. The water was calm, and

Frobisher Bay at noon in winter

Entrance to Auyuittuq in spring

Heading north to park entrance, 11:00 P.M., August 1984

Park headquarters at Overlord. Building is held down against winds up to 200 km per hour

Andrea at our first campsite

Ready to start about 5 A.M. in the land of the midnight sun

Slowed down by glacial streams

Rocks, gravel, and boulders on path brought down by glaciers

JHB enters
Arctic Circle

Looking east in Pangnirtung Pass. Rivers are fast, cold, and dangerous during summer melt.

Looking east to Highway glacier, the halfway point of pass.
We realized we were not going to reach our goal.

Opposite
Arctic cotton grass

Flora is only a few centimetres high due to lack of soil and
short growing season.

Broad-leafed willow herb

Arctic daisies

Looking south from Overlord, waiting for the tide to come in

We leave Auyuittuq

we saw no other boat traffic during the two-hour trip. At 11:00 P.M. in the land of the midnight sun the glacially sculpted u-shaped entrance was a spectacular sight, cradled by Mount Overlord (1,500 metres) on one side, Mount Aegir (only slightly lower) on the other, and the Penny Icecap in the background.

Registering at the park, we were told that there were emergency shelters with telephones every ten kilometres, and that if we were not back in five days, a search party would be sent out. We set up our tent in a sandy spot between large lichen-covered boulders from the last ice age – a far different camping area from the ones we were accustomed to in the South. Drinking water was no problem at mealtime as there were plenty of small clear-water streams, but as there was no wood at this latitude, cooking necessitated a small, solid-fuel stove for dried meat and vegetables. It was light all night and we awoke at five to start our adventure.

The summer weather in the pass alternated between clear and sunny to misty with high winds and freezing rain or snow. Fortunately, we had five perfectly clear days. Daytime temperatures during our hike were between 6 and 8 degrees Celsius, dropping to just below freezing at night.

WE BEGIN OUR HIKE

We were physically fit in our late forties and thought we could cover five or six kilometres per hour. Our goal was to reach the middle of Pangnirtung Pass (now called Aksayook Pass) following the Weasel River bed to Summit Lake – a distance of fifty kilometres – halfway to the trail end at Broughton Island on the east coast of Baffin Island. From there we would return. But hiking in the Arctic soon proved to be a very different experience from our previous treks in the South. We could only manage about three kilometres per hour. Three things slowed us down. First, on the flat we made relatively fair but physically tiring progress on soft sand and wet, spongy tundra. Second, we frequently had to climb up and down old moraines – fifty-metre high masses of gravel and boulders brought down by glaciers. The third and major impediment to our progress was the recurrent fording of very cold, grey, shallow rivers caused by the increased glacial runoff in the warm sunny days.

Every three or four kilometres we would have to stop, take off our shoes and socks, put on the running shoes hanging around our necks, and as quickly as possible walk through the freezing water over slippery stones. On the other side we would take off our running shoes and wait for five to ten minutes for our numb feet to warm up. Subsequent stream crossings were more uncomfortable because of wet running shoes. There was always a tendency to move further upstream where the rivers became narrower, but this was dangerous as they also were closer to the lip of the glacier and deeper. Fast water over the slippery bottom was likely to knock us over if it rose much above our knees. The cardinal rule was to always unbuckle the waist belt on our backpack so that it would fall off and not drag us under in any encounter with unexpected deep water.

Our first thrill was reaching an inuksuk (a cairn made of carefully piled stones, usually shaped in human form, marking a trail) with a sign in English, French, and Inuktitut indicating that we had crossed the Arctic Circle. We continued along the Weasel River valley, by mid-afternoon reaching our first campsite on its bank near Windy Lake – well named, as it turned out. On a cloudless day, surrounded by mountains and glaciers, the view was dominated by Mount Thor rising 1,500 metres above the river valley. Thor has been described as the tallest cliff in the world. It is a challenge for experienced climbers, as its steep riverside face and overlapping top have never been scaled. We were told that a team of Japanese professionals spent over a week in an unsuccessful attempt to reach the summit.

We set up our tent on flat ground near an emergency centre, surrounded by purple broad-leafed willow herb and arctic cotton grass swaying in the wind. The summer vegetation in the Weasel Valley was very colourful. Many of the plant species seemed like smaller versions of southern counterparts due to the lack of topsoil and the permafrost hampering growth. Arctic poppies covered the flatland between moraines. We did not see any larger animals such as wolverines, caribou, and polar bears, as they rarely came into the valleys, but several white Arctic hares and one fox visited our campsite over our five-day trip. Ground squirrels were numerous, but it was not a year for lemmings. Flocks of Canada Geese and the odd falcon flew overhead, and a number of Arctic Terns landed close by.

We walked on without our packs to see what lay ahead for the next day. The outlook was discouraging. The grey, silt-laden glacial streams become very rapid and deep during the brief summer melt, resulting in the Weasel River, swollen by the rising side-streams from the melting glaciers, constantly changing its course. Available crossings varied from day to day. We crossed to the north bank over a narrow wooden suspension bridge swaying alarmingly with each step and soon encountered raging torrents of water over and in between large boulders. We could see the next emergency shelter ten kilometres distant, but realized that even if we had more time before I had to be back for my clinic in Iqaluit, we could not reach our objective. We decided to return to our campsite for supper and spend the next few days on short walks enjoying the scenery.

The valley became dark below the mountain peaks, but the top third of Mount Thor remained red from the sun all night. During the middle of the night, the wind funnelled down the narrow river valley at more than one hundred kilometres an hour,

flattening our sturdy mountain tent. We admitted defeat, weighted
down our unusable tent with rocks, and spent the rest of the
night comfortably in the well-secured emergency shelter.

We saw no people until the fourth day when we met a lawyer
and an accountant from Ontario. They were pleased to have
made it to Summit Lake but had spent several days in their tent
playing cribbage during ice storms and were grateful for the improving weather. During our last night at Windy Lake we visited
with two men and a woman from San Francisco, where we had
lived fifteen years previously while I was training at the Cardiovascular Research Institute. They were experienced northern
travellers, having flown their own aircraft to various locations including the Rocky Mountains and the western Arctic. We made
coffee and watched the sun warm the top of Mount Thor as we

Emergency shelters at our first campsite

Crossing Otter River on a primitive bridge. Andrea goes first.

reminisced about San Francisco and previous camping trips. We passed them the next morning on our way out to find that their supposedly windproof tent, like ours, was no match for the wind tunnel in the Weasel River valley. We advised them to use the emergency shelter.

Our return to Overlord was even slower than the walk in because during three warm days the streams had become significantly deeper. It was suddenly colder in the early mornings, and we required toques and gloves. Thin ice covered smaller streams and after fording them it took longer for our feet to warm up. Instead of the empty campsite we found on arrival, there was now a group of tents between the rocks occupied by a Swedish cross-country skiing team going in to train on the Penny Icecap and a group of fit-looking young Japanese presumably preparing for another assault on Mount Thor.

The next morning the tide was out in the sound so we had to wait until noon for our boat ride back to Pangnirtung. As we looked out on the reflection of the mountains in the calm waters of the sound, Andrea and I vowed to return with more time available so that we could complete the one-hundred kilometre trip across the Cumberland Peninsula to Broughton Island. Unfortunately our busy lives never provided us the opportunity.

PANGNIRTUNG, GATEWAY INTO THE ARCTIC CIRCLE

Pangnirtung ("the place of the bull caribou") with its view north to the entrance of Auyittuq Park is one of the most picturesque Arctic settlements. It supports all three Inuit crafts of carving, print-making, and weaving. In 1980 these were exhibited and sold in a few small dilapidated buildings, since replaced by a modern co-operative museum and store.

Inuit children stay up and play until very late during the long daylight of summer. Andrea talked with a number of them as we

The early days of the Inuit art industry

wandered through the town, looking at sealskins stretched to dry in the sun and racks of pink Arctic char (a very tasty cold-water relative of salmon) strung in front of many houses. One small child happily chewed on a raw fish, seemingly avoiding the bones like a cat. The scene reminded us of the derivation of the word "Eskimo" – "eater of raw meat." On a few later occasions when I was invited to eat in an Inuit home, I was politely offered cooked meat.

We had been advised by my colleagues in Iqaluit not to stay in the expensive Pangnirtung hotel but to go to the Anglican Church where, for a small donation, the minister would let us sleep on the floor. This turned out to be an excellent decision. Michael Gardiner, the Anglican minister, had come to Canada from Scotland several years earlier. We watched and listened as he spoke to a group of youngsters in their language. He held their rapt attention. It was the only time I ever heard Inuktitut spoken with a Scottish accent.

Anglican church in Pangnirtung where we spent the night before returning to Iqaluit

During our visit to the park headquarters and museum in Pangnirtung we learned, among other things, the problem of post-secondary education in the Arctic. We met an intelligent and well-spoken young man about sixteen or seventeen years of age who was in training to become a park ranger. He obviously would have benefited from further education beyond high school, but that would have meant living in Iqaluit for two years. He recognized that during that time he would be exposed to smoking, alcohol, and drugs. He said to us: "I'll never go to Frob [Iqaluit]." Those few words said a lot.

The evening before our departure we visited the nursing station and talked with two nurses, Martha and Tops, who had been working together for ten years. One of the women was from Stanstead, Quebec, just north of the Quebec/Vermont border where I had been crossing all my life to a country home on Lake Memphremagog. They were planning a trip into the park in two weeks' time, so we gave them some advice regarding the rapidly

Young boys in late summer evening

Andrea talks to three young girls in Pangnirtung evening

Cemetery in Pangnirtung in late spring looking north toward entrance
to Auyuittuq Park

rising glacial rivers and left them our small cooking stove and
leftover fuel. Tragically, a few months later I received a letter in-
forming me that Tops had fallen and drowned in a river. On my
next trip to Pangnirtung the following winter I visited her grave-
site. The Inuit burial site was filled with unmarked white crosses.
The only named markers were those of Tops and an RCMP officer killed in the line of duty.

16

The Future

A century ago the Inuit were a nomadic people travelling in groups of up to fifty to a hundred in search of food – ice hunting for fish, whales, and seals throughout the year in the northern Arctic and both ice and land hunting in the central and southern regions. They had no need for capital or material goods as they had to carry small children and all their belongings on their backs or by dog sled. There was no local access to medical care or transport south. However, they had no exposure to southern infectious diseases or lifestyle (especially diet) predisposing them to the development of coronary artery disease. Between 1973 and 2003, I saw heart disease become manifest. The Inuit have developed a modern way of life and now share our diseases. There is no turning back on their interdependency, economically, socially, and for medical health care.

The Inuit dilemma is the maintenance of their traditional way of life supported by the elders versus the southern way of earning a living for the future of the young. The solution is not

southern-owned fishing and hunting camps for tourists, or mining corporations sending their profits south. It is an Inuit self-
governed territory providing careers and opportunities for the
coming generation. Nunavut needs many more like Andrew Taqtu,
Ida Karpik, and Jonah Kelly. Andrew kept working in the Nanisivik lead-zinc mine to support his family despite a severely dis-
eased heart valve. Ida Karpik did not let valvular heart disease
stop her from becoming one of the Arctic's leading artists. Jonah
Kelly continued as a broadcaster for CBC North in Iqaluit with a
mitral valve replacement and cardiac pacemaker. Young, healthy
Inuit must follow their examples to forge careers for themselves
in the North.

One-third of the approximately 45,000 Inuit in Canada are
under the age of sixteen, and one-half are under twenty-five.
Their economic future depends not only on the exploitation of
natural resources – particularly mining for minerals and drilling
for oil – but also on increased educational opportunities for the
young so they may see a future with good prospects of gainful
employment. Adolescents and young adults will continue to
smoke, abuse alcohol and drugs, and become sedentary and
obese on junk food – all potent risk factors for coronary disease
– if they see no viable future for themselves.

George Jacobsen, a former patient of mine, was the founder
of the Tower Group of companies. This construction enterprise was
instrumental in the building of Resolute Bay, the largest settlement in the High Arctic. George told me that he originally employed local Inuit as much as possible. However, he found that
when the summer weather was more conducive to hunting and
fishing, they would not turn up for work. He then switched to
bringing his labour force up from the South, resulting in wages
being taken out of the community. I saw this problem during my
stays at the inn in Pangnirtung where the meal table would be
full of southern labourers. Many construction and other busi-

ness firms continue to bring their employees from the South, taking wages and products away from the North. This situation must change as employment is essential for the Inuit to become self-sufficient.

It is well known in western countries that the prevalence of smoking, lack of physical exercise, and obesity predisposing to coronary artery disease is much higher in people with a lower socio-economic status. During the last few decades, the incidence of coronary events in North America – angina, heart attack, and sudden death – has decreased linearly with an increased educational level. Fortunately, educational facilities in the North such as those offered by the Arctic College in Iqualuit have improved, but as yet they have not led to a clear increase in employment opportunity.

The economic future of the Inuit also depends on their ability to develop and export their own natural resources. Despite the National Land Claims Agreement of 1993, this has not happened, as the Government of Canada is reluctant to give up its claim to the resources in the Arctic land and territorial waters. The federal government cannot continue to assert its sovereignty over the Northwest Passage while denying the Inuit the development of mining and oil resources in the area. George Jacobsen envisioned a year-round port in Iqaluit over two decades ago, but this still is under debate.

During the last three decades the Inuit social future has changed considerably. Southerners coming North are now more likely to stay for prolonged periods of time because of the appealing slower pace of life and improved long-term economic opportunities. I frequently awaited my plane trip home in Iqaluit with my dentist friend Marc Levesque and his wife. They were always amused by my concern about getting to the airport through a snowstorm on time. Marc would pour me another drink and tell me to wait until we heard the incoming plane roar overhead.

147

There was always plenty of time. This way of life increasingly appeals to southerners. Social interaction and intermarriage between the two cultures is leading to a better understanding of the other's way of life. The white man is no longer there just to take out wages and resources, then leave.

FUTURE HEART HEALTH

With the exception of sexually transmitted disease, which remains significantly higher in the Inuit compared to people in the South, the frequently fatal infectious diseases such as tuberculosis originally introduced by the early southern traders have largely been controlled. The Inuit now face the same degenerative diseases in middle life as the rest of the developed world.

Congenital (present at birth) heart disease will remain constant at about 1 per cent of live births. Rheumatic heart disease causing severe valvular problems in the young is almost gone as a result of the decrease in acute rheumatic fever and its recurrences by the early and widespread use of antibiotics. This leaves coronary artery disease – a more difficult problem, as it requires lifestyle changes and not just medication.

The incidence of cigarette smoking is about double in the Inuit and Indian populations compared to the rest of Canada. It has been part of the Inuit way of life since European whalers introduced it during the nineteenth century. I saw grandfathers, fathers and children lighting up together. Smoking in young children seemed equivalent to that in Southeast Asia. Obviously, the younger the age at which a person begins to smoke, the more difficult it will be to stop later. The chance of future complications also increases. Nunavut's birth rate is more than twice Canada's average – hence the necessity of addressing risk factors in the young. Most smokers fear lung cancer, but coronary heart disease is a more frequent and lethal outcome. I estimated that about three-quarters of young people over the age of ten smoked, making it the number-one public health problem in the Arctic.

Alcohol consumption, which predisposes to hypertension – an important risk factor for coronary heart disease – is also much higher in the Arctic. Fortunately, the closing of government liquor outlets and the designation of dry settlements have reduced it to some extent. However, when young people are unemployed and see no future, they are likely to spend their time smoking and drinking alcohol.

The social and economic problems of the modern Inuit lead to a high incidence of suicide, about double that in the South. I remember seeing a middle-aged woman with a heart attack in the emergency room in Kuujjuak while her adolescent son lay dead from a self-inflicted gunshot wound a few doors away. This tragic waste of life will only be solved by improving socio-economic conditions.

The Inuit diet and lack of physical activity results in obesity and the metabolic syndrome, which now equals or surpasses that in the developed world. This is the epidemic that must now be addressed. Doctors, nurses, and hospitals will not solve this problem. Improving social and economic conditions will help, but as in the rest of the developed world, a major lifestyle change is urgently needed.

17

Transitions

I was chief of Cardiology at the Montreal General Hospital from 1973 to 1994. The administrative duties were becoming more and more onerous with budget cuts and I had less time for teaching and medical writing in several journals. I decided that after twenty-one years it was time to resign as chief, but I continued my clinical and teaching duties. In 1998 the McGill-Baffin Project was terminated by the Baffin Regional Health Board and transferred to Ottawa. Leaving my many patients in the high Arctic after twenty-five years was a big disappointment, but I continued my cardiac consulting duties to northern Quebec (Nunavik) for five more years.

The most difficult time of my life came in July of 1999 when Andrea, my wife of forty-one years, was diagnosed with breast cancer. Her illness was a shock since she had always been strong and healthy and there was no family history of the disease. Andrea had breastfed all our children, which was supposed to reduce the risk of breast cancer. We were initially optimistic as the

As I remember her: Andrea and John, 1985

Andrea and John, family reunion, 2000

Family reunion, 2000

Family reunion, 2000
Christmas 2000: Jay,
Andrea, and Logan
(youngest grandchild)

Cindy, Jay, Willa, and Lynn, Vermont, 2002

tumour appeared small, and surgery was planned for after Labour Day. We did not tell our children who were visiting with their families at our country home in Vermont. The two older girls had gone to the United States for master's degrees, married Americans and now lived in Texas and California. Our son was working as an engineer on oil rigs in Indonesia. Only our third daughter was living in Montreal with her husband and daughter.

Andrea had her surgery in early September. The tumour was more extensive than expected and following surgery was found to have spread to her liver. Our children and I were totally un-prepared for this eventuality. Andrea's prognosis had changed from excellent to incurable. I had planned to call each one of our children and report that their mother had minor surgery and an excellent outlook. Instead I made four very difficult phone calls and answered all their questions as best I could. I knew they would go to the Internet and research breast cancer. None of my children chose a career in the health sciences, but they are all intelligent and thoughtful adults and had a close relationship with their mother.

Chemotherapy began with initially favourable results. I forced myself to be optimistic although I knew the outlook was poor – less than two years. We had a family reunion near Banff, Alberta, for Andrea's sixty-fifth birthday in October 2000 with our four children, three sons-in-law, and six grandchildren. We were at a hotel 4,000 kilometres from home when Andrea's hip suddenly broke because the cancer had spread to her bones. She refused to cut the reunion short despite her pain. She was in a wheelchair for two days until we returned to Montreal to have the hip repaired. She again recovered and resumed her activities, including her presidency of the Atwater Library. Two months later she staggered and fell in our living room. She lay on the floor unable to get up. The tumour had spread to her brain. We spent Christmas in Vermont, and in January Andrea was admitted to palliative care at the MGH. I tried to resume my normal duties at the hospital and visited her three or four times daily. I found it frustrating that although I could help my own patients, I could do nothing for her. It was devastating to watch her slowly deteriorate over the next five months. She died 29 April 2001. I had lost my lifelong companion. We had done everything together, and I could not imagine life without her. I took a three-month leave of absence and went to our country home, spending the summer with my children and grandchildren.

I returned to my clinical and teaching duties in September and gradually adapted to living alone. It was very difficult for me to continue my life without Andrea. She had always been there to support my career. I missed the little things like calling home every day at noon to find out how her day was going and share my news with her. She had been at the centre of our family, the person who always knew where everything was, and the link that held us together. After she died, I made an effort to regularly email my children and phone them every Sunday from our country home in Vermont. I visited my daughters in the United States over Christmas – they did not want me to be alone.

In February 2002 my life suddenly changed again. While walking home from the hospital, I slipped and fell on some ice, fracturing my pelvis. This required a five-hour surgery to repair the bones with plates and screws, followed by eight weeks of non-weight bearing in a convalescent home. After so many years of caring for other people in hospital, I found myself a patient in a hospital bed.

One night at the convalescent hospital as I was getting into bed to watch a movie, I suddenly found myself so short of breath that I could barely talk. I knew immediately I had a large pulmonary embolism (clot to the lungs) – nothing else could explain the acuteness and severity of my breathing problem. I rang for the nurse. She told me that I was panicking and should relax. I gasped that I was not prone to panic attacks. I had sustained a major pulmonary embolism, and she needed to arrange for oxygen, an electrocardiogram, and an ambulance.

The staff soon realized something was wrong when my pulse rate rose to 180 and my blood pressure and oxygen saturation fell. A doctor appeared and did an electrocardiogram. He said everything was fine. I motioned for him to give me the tracing, which confirmed my diagnosis. I was sure I was going to die. Fortunately, by the time the ambulance got me to the emergency room of the Montreal General Hospital, my breathing was better and my pulse rate slowing. The ER doctor was a former student of mine. I asked him to immediately start heparin (a rapid-acting blood thinner to prevent further lung clots) before waiting for the results of a CAT scan. This confirmed my diagnosis. Two of my five lung lobes were completely blocked by clot, and a third was partially obstructed. Now another urgent decision had to be made – whether to give me a powerful thrombolytic (clot-dissolving) drug, a treatment of uncertain value especially in view of my stabilizing condition, or to continue with conservative treatment. The use of a thrombolytic drug was risky as it could cause serious bleeding at the site of my recent operation. Dr Ash Gursahaney, the director of Intensive Care, made the correct decision against thrombolysis. He played the major role in saving my life. During the next few days I again experienced the life of a patient. Dr Gursahaney brought students to see me – I was an interesting case.

I recovered slowly and gradually resumed walking with a cane. I returned to work and even made one more trip to northern Quebec. However, for the first time in my life I was worried about the ice and scared of falling on the hard snow. I had difficulty climbing into a Twin Otter. My hip discomfort and lack of mobility convinced my colleagues, children, and myself that I should give up my clinical practice and semi-retire to teaching and writing. This proved to be the right decision, especially as it gave me the time to write about my experiences in the Arctic and to evaluate the many influences that led me to dedicate my life to the study of heart disease.

My thirty years of Arctic cardiology provided me with the most rewarding part of my clinical career. My training for an academic career in medicine both in Birmingham, England, and at the University of California, San Francisco, involved working closely with senior and junior colleagues, experience in teaching at the undergraduate and postgraduate levels, and learning to use state-of-the art diagnostic equipment. My practice of cardiology in the Arctic, on the other hand, required the use of purely bedside skills – talking to patients to obtain a history of their illness, depending upon my hands, eyes, and ears with very little technology. In the North many family doctors stayed for only short periods, and so I was the only long-term physician for many patients. Perhaps most importantly, I had no specialist colleagues to consult in deciding on a diagnosis and course of treatment. I felt I was helping more in the North than in my Montreal practice. It was cardiology in the trenches and made me appreciate how much responsibility was required of the family physicians and nurses in the North. It was an honour to help them with their patient care and provide them with teaching sessions, both during my visits and by fax and telephone in between.

My experiences in the North not only reinforced my belief in the value of bedside medicine as compared to too much reliance on technology but also gave me a profound appreciation of one of the world's most unique aboriginal people. Watching John Wayne movies and reading books do not provide an understanding of the American Indian. Few people have the opportunity to become immersed, even for short periods, in a culture very different from their own. My northern visits allowed me to meet many Inuit and learn their history and culture. I also realized how isolated a patient must feel when transported to a hospital in a different place for a major operation, particularly when exposed to a different language. It was rewarding to see their faces light up in recognition when I visited them at the MGH.

I saw coronary heart disease appear and progress during my thirty years in the Arctic. This reinforced my belief in the importance of lifestyle as the cause of many diseases and of its change, rather than drugs, in their prevention. Doctors must treat the whole patient and not just complaints and diseases. This requires a close bond with many people each day and resulted in my interest in the history and culture of the Inuit. I have learned a lot from books over the years, but I learned more from talking to my patients, their families, and other health care providers.

The great American philosopher George Santayana (1863–1952), wrote: "Those who cannot remember the past are condemned to repeat it." I remember nearly every moment of my career as an Arctic cardiologist and wish that I could repeat it.

Notes

1 W.B. Kouwenhoven, J.R. Jude, and G.G. Knickerbocker, "Closed-Chest Cardiac Massage," *Journal of the American Medical Association* 173 (1960): 1064–7.
2 R.E. Fossett, *In Order to Live Untroubled* (Winnipeg: University of Manitoba Press, 2001), 223.
3 J. Diamond, *Guns, Germs and Steel* (New York: W.W. Norton, 1999), 224–38.
4 Ibid., 256.
5 R. McGhee, *The Last Imaginary Place* (Toronto: Key Porter, 2004), 93.
6 J. Diamond, *Collapse* (New York: Viking Penguin, 2005), 255–65.
7 R. McGhee, *The Last Imaginary Place*, 102.
8 Ibid., 126.
9 Ibid., 103.
10 Cited in K.J. Crowe, *A History of the Original Peoples of Northern Canada* (Montreal: McGill-Queen's University Press, 1974), 168–9.
11 Ibid.

12 Canada, Department of Mines and Resources, *The Book of Wisdom for Eskimo* (Ottawa), 1947.

13 O. Schaefer, *Health Problems and Health Care Delivery in the Canadian North. Northern Health Research Unit* (Winnipeg: University of Manitoba, 1993), 27.

14 J. Bennett and S. Rowley, eds., *Uqalurait: An Oral History of Nunavut* (Kingston and Montreal: McGill-Queen's University Press, 2004), 176.

15 Ibid.

16 J. Diamond, *Guns, Germs and Steel*, 202–10.

17 K.J. Crowe, *A History of the Original Peoples of Northern Canada*, 178.

18 J. Bennett and S. Rowley, eds., *Uqalurait*, 4-7.

19 J. Wolkowicz and J.H. Burgess, "Complete Heart Block in an Inuit Family," *Canadian Journal of Cardiology* 4, no. 7 (1988): 352–4.

20 M.J. McLaren, M. Markowitz, and M.A. Gerber, "Rheumatic Heart Disease in Developing Countries: The Consequences of Inadequate Prevention," *Annals of Internal Medicine* 120 (1994): 243–5.

21 M. Hill, *Nunatsiaq News*, 17 May 2002, 12–13.

22 Ibid.

23 W. Steger and P. Schurke, *North to the Pole* (New York: Times Books, 1987).

24 O. Schaefer, R.D.P. Eaton, F.J.W. Timmermans, and J.A. Hildes, "Respiratory Function Impairment and Cardiopulmonary Consequences in Long-Term Residents of the Canadian Arctic," *Canadian Medical Association Journal* 123 (1980): 997–1004.

25 A. Bertelsen, "Gronlansk medicinsk statistik of nosgraft," *Medd Grönland* 117 (1935): 1–83.

26 T.K. Young, M.E. Moffatt, and J.D. O'Neil, "Cardiovascular Diseases in a Canadian Arctic Population," *American Journal of Public Health* 83 (1993): 881–7.

27 P. Bjerregaard, T.K. Young, and R.A. Hegele, "Low Incidence of Cardiovascular Disease among the Inuit – What Is the Evidence?" *Atherosclerosis* 166 (2003): 351–7.

28 G.W. Hawkins, "Schaefer of the Arctic," *Annals of the RCPSC* 35 (2002): 173–6.

29 E. Dewailly C. Blanchet, S. Lemieux, L. Sauvé, S. Gingras, P. Ayotte, and B.J. Holub, "N-3 Fatty Acids and Cardiovascular Risk Factors among the Inuit of Nunavik, *American Journal of Clinical Nutrition* 74 (2001): 464–73.

30 I.M. Rabinowitch, "Clinical and Other Observations on Canadian Eskimos in the Eastern Arctic," *Canadian Medical Association Journal* 34 (1936): 498.

31 Ibid., 487–501.

32 Ibid., 498.

33 H.M. Sinclair, "The Diet of Canadian Indians and Eskimos," *Proceedings of the Nutrition Society* 12, no. 1 (1953): 69–82.

34 T.R. Dawber, *The Framingham Study* (Cambridge, Mass.: Harvard University Press, 1980).

35 A. Keys, *Seven Countries* (Cambridge, Mass.: Harvard University Press, 1980).

Index

Aber, Geoff, 22
Addis Ababa, 101
alcohol consumption, 56, 149
angina, 122
aortic insufficiency, 109
apex, 114
Arctic Bay, 72
Arctic College, 80
Arctic Small Tool Tradition 62
Arnott, Melville, 22
art, Inuit, 56–8, 103–4
Auyittuq, 133

Baffin-Hudson Strait, 67
Baragwanth Hospital, South
  Africa, 101
Bering Straits migration, 59

Birmingham, England, Queen
  Elizabeth Hospital, 22, 25, 101
Bishop, John, 23, 28, 29, 30
Book of Wisdom for Eskimo, 71
British Medical Research Society,
  30
Broughton Island, 58, 84, 135
Burgess, Andrea C., 13–14, 133,
  139–43, 150–6; wedding, 17
Burgess, Cynthia A., 32
Burgess, J. Lynn, 38
Burgess, Jay F., 41
Burgess, John Frederick, 3, 4,
  8–10
Burgess, Reta, 4, 9, 10–12, 18, 31
Burgess, Willa C., 30

Cameron, Douglas G., 20, 21, 22, 33, 47

Cape Dorset, 58, 89, 93

cardiac arrest, Code 99, 34

cardiomyopathy, 118

cardiomyoplasty, and Ray C.J. Chui, 120–1

Cardiovascular Research Institute, San Francisco, 36

C.D. Howe, 81

cholesterol, high and low density, 125

Cindy, 96

closed chest massage, 27

Cole, Sam and Jane, 38

Coman, Fred, 56

complete heart block, 88

Comroe, Julius H. Jr., 36

congenital and inherited disease, 85

Cree, 67

Cronin, R.F. Patrick, 33, 40, 42, 45

Cumberland Sound, 67, 79

cyanotic and non-cyanotic congenital heart disease, 87

Daisy, 118, 119

dental hygiene, 112–13

Diane, 108

diffusing capacity, 28

Dorset People, 62

double valve replacement, 100

Duff, Lyman, 13

Duthie, George Ian, 7

Emily, 106, 107

Eskimo, 59

Eskimo Book of Knowledge, 70

Ferguson, George V., 22

Fleming, Andrew Lang, 79

Forsey, R.R., 20

Framingham Study, 123, 128

Frobisher, Martin, 66

Frobisher Bay, 48, 74, 81

Gardiner, Michael, 141

graduation, J.H.B., 16

Grise Fiord, 72

Gursahaney, Ash, 157

Hadjis, Tom, 95

Harris, Peter, 23

heart attack monitoring, 27

Hudson Bay Company, 69–70, 79, 127

Hurteau, Gilles, 45

internship and residency training, MGH, 18, 32

Inukjuak, 55, 115

Inuksuk, 136

Inuktitut, 51, 61

Iou, Pia, 98

Iqaluit, 48, 54

Jacobsen, George, 146, 147
Joe, 119, 120
Johanassie, 105, 106, 107
Jones, Di, and Norman, 39

Karpik, Ida, 103–4, 146
kayak, 63
Kelly, Jonah, 92, 146
Kuujjuak, 48, 54, 80, 81

Leblond, C.P., 12
Levesque, Marc, 113, 147
Livingston, David, 79

Martha, 142
Martin, C.P., 11
McGill-Baffin Project, 82, 91
McGill Medical School, 10, 11
McGinness, Willa Reta, 4, 9
measles, 79
Medical Research Council
  Scholarship, 40
metabolic syndrome, 130
mitral insufficiency, 102
mitral stenosis, 96, 97
mitral valve disease, 26
Mongolia, 59, 66
Montreal Children's Hospital, 84
Montreal Gazette, 17, 38
Mount Thor, 136

Nadel, Jay, 38
Nala, 109

Nanisivik, 72, 97
Nascopie, 81, 126
Norse, 62
Nuffield Traveling Fellowship, 22
Nunavik, 48, 72
Nunavut, 47

obesity, 130, 149
Ojibway Hotel 15
Order of Canada, 110
Osler, Sir William, 14
Overlord, 134

pacemakers, 26
Pangnirtung, 53, 58, 76, 81, 104,
  140–4
Pangnirtung Pass, 135
Paton, Pauline, 80
Penny Icecap, 135
Pond Inlet, 115
Puvirnituq, 48,81

R.S. McLaughlin Fellowship 36
Rabinowitch, I.M., 123, 128
Rapaport, Elliot, 38
Reid, E.A.A.S, 33, 34
rheumatic fever, 97–8, 101–2
Rouleau, J.L., 42
Royal College Exams, 33
Royal College of Physicians and
  Surgeons of Canada, 42

Salluit, 54

Santayana, George, 159
Schaeffer, Otto, 79, 116, 117, 125
Seidman, Christine, 72
Seven Country Study, 128
shamans, 76–8, 83
Sinclair, H.M., 127, 128
small group teaching, 28
smallpox, 78
smoking, cigarette, 116–17, 148–9
Stanley, Mary and Eric, 23
Summit Lake, 135

Taqtu, Andrew, 97, 146
Thompson, Alan, 20
thrombolytic treatment, 131, 132
Thule, 64
Tops, 142, 144
tricuspid insufficiency, 104

Tristan da Cuhna, 112
tuberculosis, 79
Tunit, 62
typhoid fever, 79

umiaks, 64
U.S. Air Force, 72

viral diseases, 78

Warnica, Wayne, 42
Watt, Daisy, 86
Weasel River, 136, 137
Weinberg, Hershie, 52
White, Paul Dudley, 14
Williams Syndrome, 106–7
Wolfe-Parkinson-White Syndrome, 93
Wolkowicz, Joel, 91
Woodhouse, Professor, 8